Issues
Annual Index
2006

ISSUES

Compiled by
Ann Shooter

Independence
Educational Publishers
Cambridge

First published by Independence
PO Box 295
Cambridge CB1 3XP

ISBN 1 86168 373 1

Printed in Great Britain
MWL Print Group Ltd

Layout by
Lisa Firth

A

abattoirs **19**.25, 26, 28
abdominal obesity, health risks **113**.11, 15
abductions by terrorists **92**.9
abortion
    access to abortions **126**.24
    after-effects **126**.10, 11, 14
    arguments against (pro-life) **126**.21-2, 25
    arguments for (pro-choice) **126**.21
    clinics **126**.12
    confidentiality **126**.13, 28, 29, 30
    costs **126**.12
    deaths from **20**.25, 27, 30
    decision-making **126**.9-10, 12-13
    men **126**.15-16
    young people **126**.17-18
    and depression **126**.11
    early medical abortion **126**.14, 33
    and emergency contraception (the morning after pill) **126**.24
    ethical considerations **126**.21-2
    and foetal abnormality **126**.9, 34, 35
    home abortions **126**.32-4
    and humanism **126**.4-5
    late abortion **126**.14, 37-8
    and the law **126**.5, 6, 7-8, 12
    and men **126**.15-16
    methods
        medical abortion ('the abortion pill') **126**.10, 14, 32-4
        vacuum aspiration ('the suction method') **126**.10, 14
    reasons for abortions **126**.8, 9, 21
    foetal abnormality **126**.9, 34, 35
    late abortions **126**.37
    religious positions on **126**.1-3, 6
    risks **126**.10, 14
    home abortions **126**.32, 34
    statistics **126**.18
    and teenage pregnancies **20**.30, 34; **75**.1, 3, 4, 17; **126**.29
    under 16s **126**.13, 28, 29
    time limit **126**.12, 36-8
abrupt climate change **95**.17-20
absenteeism **107**.6-8, 18
    and obesity **113**.17
abstinence education **75**.18, 26-7
abusive relationships
    and self-harm **77**.10, 14
    and young runaways **79**.25, 29
academic freedom **121**.8-9
access audits **91**.10-11, 14, 15-16
accident warning devices, cars **119**.19
accidents
    alcohol-related **123**.16
    child labour and work-related **99**.1
    compensation, and same-sex partnerships **101**.30-1
    and older people **105**.5
    road accidents, children **119**.5, 28, 30-31
    and young travellers **109**.12, 14-15
achievement, black pupils **115**.20
acid rain **76**.11
acne **123**.28
    and milk consumption **19**.18
active euthanasia **102**.1, 2
active traffic management **119**.37-8
activity
    as help for depression **125**.3, 39
    and improving self-esteem **117**.6, 8, 33
acupressure **81**.1, 3
acupuncture **81**.5-6, 14, 23, 36; **86**.30, 37
addictions **123**.8
    drugs **114**.5, 17-18
    nicotine **123**.12
    signs **123**.14
administration method and drug effects **114**.2
admissions, school, gender equality **112**.9
adoption
    as alternative to abortion **126**.24
    and children's rights **120**.11
adult children
    parental interference **124**.14-15
    supported by parents **124**.3

Volume numbers appear first (in bold) followed by page numbers; a change in volume number is preceded by a semi-colon.

Vol. **19** Looking at Vegetarianism
Vol. **20** Population Growth
Vol. **22** Confronting Child Abuse
Vol. **29** Gambling
Vol. **43** A Consumer Society
Vol. **60** Confronting Cancer
Vol. **69** The Media
Vol. **74** Money Matters
Vol. **75** Lone-Parent Families
Vol. **76** The Water Crisis
Vol. **77** Self-inflicted Violence
Vol. **78** Threatened Species
Vol. **79** Dealing with Homelessness
Vol. **80** The Cannabis Debate
Vol. **81** Alternative Therapies
Vol. **82** Protecting our Privacy
Vol. **83** Dealing with Crime
Vol. **84** Mental Wellbeing
Vol. **85** The Housing Crisis
Vol. **86** Smoking and your Health
Vol. **87** Genetic Modification

Vol. **88** Food and Nutrition
Vol. **89** Refugees
Vol. **90** Human and Animal Cloning
Vol. **91** Disability Issues
Vol. **92** Terrorism
Vol. **93** Binge Drinking
Vol. **94** Religions and Beliefs in Britain
Vol. **95** The Climate Crisis
Vol. **96** Preventing Sexual Diseases
Vol. **97** Energy Matters
Vol. **98** The Globalisation Issue
Vol. **99** Exploited Children
Vol. **100** Stress and Anxiety
Vol. **101** Sexuality and Discrimination
Vol. **102** The Ethics of Euthanasia
Vol. **103** Animal Rights
Vol. **104** Our Internet Society
Vol. **105** Ageing Issues
Vol. **106** Trends in Marriage
Vol. **107** Work Issues
Vol. **108** Domestic Violence

Vol. **109** Responsible Tourism
Vol. **110** Poverty
Vol. **111** The Waste Problem
Vol. **112** Women, Men and Equality
Vol. **113** Fitness and Health
Vol. **114** Drug Abuse
Vol. **115** Racial Discrimination
Vol. **116** Grief and Loss
Vol. **117** Self-Esteem and Body Image
Vol. **118** Focus on Sport
Vol. **119** Transport Trends
Vol. **120** The Human Rights Issue
Vol. **121** The Censorship Debate
Vol. **122** Bullying
Vol. **123** Young People and Health
Vol. **124** Parenting Issues
Vol. **125** Understanding Depression
Vol. **126** The Abortion Debate
Vol. **127** Eating Disorders

adult deaths from AIDS, impact on children **110**.37
adult literacy rates, and child labour **99**.11-12
adults
    consequences of childhood bullying **122**.6
    participation in sports **118**.1
advance directives (living wills) **102**.18, 29, 32, 33-9
adventure travel **109**.9-10
advertising **69**.11-15, 28-30
    alcohol **93**.2
    and body image **117**.18
    British meat **19**.4, 40
    and children **43**.6, 7, 8, 9; **69**.11-13, 14
    cigarettes and tobacco **86**.5, 8, 26
    cinema **69**.30
    direct mail **69**.29
    junk food **88**.10, 11, 19, 20, 35, 37
    and childhood obesity **113**.2
    leaflet distribution **69**.29
    in magazines **69**.14, 28-9
    in newspapers **69**.28-9
    radio **69**.21, 28
    and sex discrimination **112**.14
    television **69**.3, 12, 26, 29
aerobic exercise **113**.22
aerosol cans recycling **111**.36
affirmation and self-confidence **117**.34
affordable housing **79**.1, 2, 9, 11-12, 35; **85**.29-31
    and the exception site policy **85**.28
    giving public money to private developers **85**.19
    and homelessness **79**.1, 2, 9, 11-12, 35
    and housing associations **85**.19
    large houses **85**.11
    policies **85**.28-30
    and public sector workers **85**.1, 3, 4, 20, 21, 22
    in rural areas **85**.5, 28, 31
    shortage of **85**.1, 3, 8-9, 20
    and social housing **85**.8
    and young workers **85**.3-4
African-Caribbean people **115**.5
    pupils, exclusion **115**.19
age
    and adventure travel **109**.9
and alcohol consumption **123**.16-17
and attitudes to advertising **69**.14
and attitudes to illegal drugs **80**.27-8
and breast cancer **60**.23
and child labour **99**.2
and child soldiers **99**.29-30
of children and divorcing parents **106**.33-4; **124**.33-4
and children's rights **120**.1,2
and contraception **75**.15
of criminal responsibility **83**.29-30; **120**.12
and dementia **84**.11, 12
of divorce **106**.3, 23, 25, 26
of first cohabitation **106**.10
and first-time house buyers **85**.7
and gambling **29**.2, 8, 27, 34-5, 35-6
and Internet access **69**.3
and Internet safety **104**.22-3
and Internet shopping **104**.7
and Internet use **104**.12
of lone parents **75**.28; **106**.3
of marriage **106**.3, 25
of missing persons **79**.13
of retirement **105**.20, 27
of self-harmers **77**.6
of smokers **86**.1
and stress levels **100**.13
and suicide rates **77**.2, 17
and television viewing **69**.2, 4
of young offenders **83**.15
voting age lowering **120**.7-8
age of consent **99**.25-6; **101**.27
age discrimination **110**.19-20
age ratings
    films **121**.23-5, 29-30
    video games **121**.32-3
ageing
    benefits of exercise **113**.22
    genetic engineering and the postponement of **105**.31-3
    and the longevity revolution **105**.35-6
ageing population **20**.4, 5, 9, 33; **43**.3; **75**.29
    in developing countries **20**.9, 11
    and the pension crisis **105**.19, 25, 26

Volume numbers appear first (in bold) followed by page numbers; a change in volume number is preceded by a semi-colon.

Vol. **19** Looking at Vegetarianism
Vol. **20** Population Growth
Vol. **22** Confronting Child Abuse
Vol. **29** Gambling
Vol. **43** A Consumer Society
Vol. **60** Confronting Cancer
Vol. **69** The Media
Vol. **74** Money Matters
Vol. **75** Lone-Parent Families
Vol. **76** The Water Crisis
Vol. **77** Self-inflicted Violence
Vol. **78** Threatened Species
Vol. **79** Dealing with Homelessness
Vol. **80** The Cannabis Debate
Vol. **81** Alternative Therapies
Vol. **82** Protecting our Privacy
Vol. **83** Dealing with Crime
Vol. **84** Mental Wellbeing
Vol. **85** The Housing Crisis
Vol. **86** Smoking and your Health
Vol. **87** Genetic Modification

Vol. **88** Food and Nutrition
Vol. **89** Refugees
Vol. **90** Human and Animal Cloning
Vol. **91** Disability Issues
Vol. **92** Terrorism
Vol. **93** Binge Drinking
Vol. **94** Religions and Beliefs in Britain
Vol. **95** The Climate Crisis
Vol. **96** Preventing Sexual Diseases
Vol. **97** Energy Matters
Vol. **98** The Globalisation Issue
Vol. **99** Exploited Children
Vol. **100** Stress and Anxiety
Vol. **101** Sexuality and Discrimination
Vol. **102** The Ethics of Euthanasia
Vol. **103** Animal Rights
Vol. **104** Our Internet Society
Vol. **105** Ageing Issues
Vol. **106** Trends in Marriage
Vol. **107** Work Issues
Vol. **108** Domestic Violence

Vol. **109** Responsible Tourism
Vol. **110** Poverty
Vol. **111** The Waste Problem
Vol. **112** Women, Men and Equality
Vol. **113** Fitness and Health
Vol. **114** Drug Abuse
Vol. **115** Racial Discrimination
Vol. **116** Grief and Loss
Vol. **117** Self-Esteem and Body Image
Vol. **118** Focus on Sport
Vol. **119** Transport Trends
Vol. **120** The Human Rights Issue
Vol. **121** The Censorship Debate
Vol. **122** Bullying
Vol. **123** Young People and Health
Vol. **124** Parenting Issues
Vol. **125** Understanding Depression
Vol. **126** The Abortion Debate
Vol. **127** Eating Disorders

and replacement migration **20**.15, 16
services for the **20**.34-5
statistics **105**.4, 19
ageism
    and employment **105**.4, 16-27
    and health discrimination **105**.17
    legislation on age discrimination **105**.18, 20, 23-4, 26
    and older women **105**.16, 21-2
    and young people **105**.16, 24
agoraphobia **84**.16
agriculture
    and bioenergy **97**.18
    and child labour **99**.1, 2, 4
    and climate change **95**.3, 7, 9, 11, 12, 14, 15, 25, 26
    coffee growers **98**.13, 17
    cotton farming **98**.24
    energy crops **95**.29
    farm-retail price gap **98**.28
    farming productivity **87**.15, 23-4
    and food nutrition **88**.31-4
    free trade in agriculture **88**.33
    and global water shortages **76**.3, 4, 8
    and globalisation **98**.5-6, 15-16
    land degradation **20**.3, 8, 9, 13, 14, 23, 24
    and new house-building **85**.28, 33
    and population growth **20**.1, 8
    productivity **87**.15, 23-4
    seed saving **87**.29, 30
    subsidies **98**.10, 17
    and water management **76**.18, 36
    and water pollution **76**.11
    WTO trade rules **98**.21
    see also farmers; genetically modified (GM) crops
agrifood TNCs **98**.28-9, 30
aid **98**.3; **110**.28
    public opinions on **110**.34
AIDS (Acquired Immune Deficiency Syndrome) **96**.7,
        17-22, 36-9
    and child labour **99**.3
    and child soldiers **99**.31
    effect on children **110**.37
    deaths from **96**.36
    in developing countries **20**.20, 34
    education programmes **96**.32
    global funding **96**.39
    global statistics **96**.17-18, 24, 30, 36, 38
    and medical research **103**.12, 13
    orphans **96**.39
    pandemic **96**.31
    and parents of lesbians and gays **101**.17
    and population growth **20**.3, 5, 7, 11
    prevention programmes **20**.25, 27, 28, 30, 37
    and sex education **75**.21, 22
    and the sexual exploitation of children **99**.24
    tackling stigma and discrimination **96**.19, 39
    treatments **96**.18, 20
        antiretroviral therapy (ART) **96**.36, 37, 38, 39
        fixed dose combinations (FDCs) **96**.37
        vaccines **96**.33-4
    UK statistics **96**.20-2
    and young people **96**.24-6, 29

see also HIV (Human Immunodeficiency Virus)
air pollution **95**.27
    and transport **119**.1, 15, 16, 31
air travel
    airport surveillance **120**.34
    carbon dioxide emissions from **97**.25
    and global tourism **109**.2
    and global warming **109**.19
    and pollution **119**.16
    and privacy rights **82**.3
    and responsible tourism **109**.18
    and terrorism
        basic advice **92**.39
        fear of **92**.3, 4, 13
        prohibited items **92**.39
        security measures **92**.32
    terrorist attacks using aircraft **92**.9, 11
    and UK travel trends **109**.4
    women pilots **112**.27
al-Qaeda **92**.2, 8, 9, 11, 12, 14, 17-18; **94**.10
    and counter-terrorism in the UK **92**.30, 34
    and bin Laden **92**.18
    media coverage of **92**.23
    and suicide attacks **92**.16
    training camps **92**.18
alcohol **88**.7, 24; **114**.4; **123**.14-19
    and accidents **123**.16
    alcopops **93**.3, 11, 15, 23
    and anti-social behaviour **93**.23, 24, 31
    beer and lager **93**.3, 4, 5, 8
    and brain function **93**.26
    calories in **93**.3
    and cancer **60**.1, 15
    and cannabis **80**.8-9, 21
    consumption, young people **123**.1-2, 9, 18-19
    deaths related to **80**.10; **93**.8-9, 11, 18, 31, 35, 37
    and depression **125**.2, 3, 36-7
    drinks industry
        and the alcohol harm reduction strategy **93**.35
        labelling alcohol levels **93**.36
        and under-age drinking **93**.36
    and drugs **93**.33; **114**.16, 17
    effects of **93**.6-7, 13; **123**.15-16, 18; **125**.37
    as food weakness **113**.14
    government policies on
        Alcohol Harm Reduction Strategy **93**.1, 5, 10, 15,
            24, 31, 33, 35, 36
    health benefits of **93**.9, 28, 30
    health risks of **93**.4, 7, 8-9, 18, 26, 28
        and the law **114**.31
    and life expectancy **105**.2, 9-10, 29, 31
    and mental illness **84**.3, 27
    and the night-time economy **93**.2, 24
    and other drugs **80**.26
    and religion **94**.10
    responsible drinking **93**.27
        as self-medication for mental health problems **125**.36-7
    sensible drinking tips **93**.29-30
    spirits **93**.3, 4, 5, 8
    strength **123**.16
    and stress **100**.27, 31, 37, 39

support groups **123**.17
UK legislation on the sale of **93**.11; **114**.31
underage drinking **125**.9
units of **93**.4, 13, 38
and heavy drinking **93**.18
safe limits **93**.2, 3, 4, 10, 27, 29, 38
wine **93**.3, 4, 5, 8
see also binge drinking; young people and alcohol
alcohol abuse **93**.28-39
advice and support **93**.38
alternatives to alcohol **93**.34
changing habits **93**.28
children of alcoholics **93**.30, 32-3
and children and young people in prison **83**.23
costs of **93**.15, 31
cutting down on underage drinking **83**.35-6
dealing with alcohol problems **93**.28
doctors and the treatment of alcoholics **93**.31
drugs for detoxification **93**.28
expenditure on treating alcohol dependency **93**.36
fixing alcohol prices **93**.36
getting help **93**.28
and homelessness **79**.2, 7, 10, 15, 16
knowing if you have a problem **93**.30
and older people **105**.38
and self-harm **77**.10, 13, 24
and suicide **77**.3, 4, 23
tackling under-age drinking **93**.36
and teenage sex **75**.18
and yob-culture Britain **83**.5
and young offenders **83**.15
alcoholic poisoning **93**.29
alcolocks **119**.8-9
allergenicity of GM crops **87**.8, 17, 18, 19-20
alternative burials **116**.36, 38
aluminium recycling **111**.11, 23-4, 26
Alzheimer's disease **84**.11-12; **86**.11; **105**.3, 29, 37
and diet **125**.12
amenorrhea **113**.23
ammonia **86**.4, 10
amphibians
and evolution **78**.1

and the exotic pet trade **78**.21
amputations **86**.10
anabolic agents/steroids **114**.29
and the law **114**.32; **118**.35, 36
anaemia, and iron deficiency **19**.5
anaesthesia, and animal experiments **103**.6, 8, 9, 12, 22
analgesics **114**.29
Anarchist terrorist groups **92**.7
androstenedione (andro) **118**.35
anger
and bereavement **116**.4, 8, 19
and traumatic bereavement **116**.11
anger management **108**.2
for bullies **122**.18
Anglicanism **94**.1
angling **103**.30
and mental well-being **117**.38
animal cloning **90**.2, 15, 26-39
and animal welfare **90**.35
birth defects **90**.27, 28, 31, 34, 35, 39
birth weight problems **90**.27-8, 35
endangered species **90**.21, 30
ethics of **90**.29-30, 33
farm animals **90**.30, 39
for food **90**.39
health of cloned animals **90**.27, 28, 31, 34, 39
history of **90**.27
medical value to people **90**.34
for milk proteins **90**.29-30, 32, 35
pets **90**.30, 37, 38-9
procedure **90**.27, 32, 35, 36
religious views **90**.29
sporting animals **90**.30
for xeno-transplantation **90**.30, 32-3, 35
animal cruelty **103**.32-9
and abuse **103**.32
and animal welfare law **103**.33-5
education in preventing **103**.35
and the fur trade **103**.36-9
statistics **103**.34-5
animal experiments **103**.1-23
alternatives to **103**.7, 9, 10, 13-14, 17-19, 22, 23

Volume numbers appear first (in bold) followed by page numbers; a change in volume number is preceded by a semi-colon.
Vol. **19** Looking at Vegetarianism
Vol. **20** Population Growth
Vol. **22** Confronting Child Abuse
Vol. **29** Gambling
Vol. **43** A Consumer Society
Vol. **60** Confronting Cancer
Vol. **69** The Media
Vol. **74** Money Matters
Vol. **75** Lone-Parent Families
Vol. **76** The Water Crisis
Vol. **77** Self-inflicted Violence
Vol. **78** Threatened Species
Vol. **79** Dealing with Homelessness
Vol. **80** The Cannabis Debate
Vol. **81** Alternative Therapies
Vol. **82** Protecting our Privacy
Vol. **83** Dealing with Crime
Vol. **84** Mental Wellbeing
Vol. **85** The Housing Crisis
Vol. **86** Smoking and your Health
Vol. **87** Genetic Modification
Vol. **88** Food and Nutrition
Vol. **89** Refugees
Vol. **90** Human and Animal Cloning
Vol. **91** Disability Issues
Vol. **92** Terrorism
Vol. **93** Binge Drinking
Vol. **94** Religions and Beliefs in Britain
Vol. **95** The Climate Crisis
Vol. **96** Preventing Sexual Diseases
Vol. **97** Energy Matters
Vol. **98** The Globalisation Issue
Vol. **99** Exploited Children
Vol. **100** Stress and Anxiety
Vol. **101** Sexuality and Discrimination
Vol. **102** The Ethics of Euthanasia
Vol. **103** Animal Rights
Vol. **104** Our Internet Society
Vol. **105** Ageing Issues
Vol. **106** Trends in Marriage
Vol. **107** Work Issues
Vol. **108** Domestic Violence
Vol. **109** Responsible Tourism
Vol. **110** Poverty
Vol. **111** The Waste Problem
Vol. **112** Women, Men and Equality
Vol. **113** Fitness and Health
Vol. **114** Drug Abuse
Vol. **115** Racial Discrimination
Vol. **116** Grief and Loss
Vol. **117** Self-Esteem and Body Image
Vol. **118** Focus on Sport
Vol. **119** Transport Trends
Vol. **120** The Human Rights Issue
Vol. **121** The Censorship Debate
Vol. **122** Bullying
Vol. **123** Young People and Health
Vol. **124** Parenting Issues
Vol. **125** Understanding Depression
Vol. **126** The Abortion Debate
Vol. **127** Eating Disorders

clinical studies **103**.7, 18, 22
computer research **103**.13-14, 17, 19, 22
epidemiology (population studies) **103**.17, 18, 19, 22
reasons for not using **103**.19
reasons for using **103**.19
tissue and cell cultures **103**.14, 17-18, 19, 22
and animal rights activists **103**.2, 9
and the anti-vivisection belief system **103**.22-3
arguments against **103**.2, 5-7
arguments for **103**.2, 9
benefits of in scientific research **103**.3
cosmetic testing **103**.23
and cruelty **103**.6-7, 9, 22
and fears of endangering patients **103**.21
and genetic research **103**.11
and genetically modified animals **103**.1, 8
and the law **103**.16, 20
and medical advances **103**.10-11
and moral justification **103**.7
questions and answers on **103**.10-11
regulation of **103**.1-2, 16, 20, 21
replacement of **103**.9
statistics **103**.1, 4, 8
and toxicological procedures **103**.8, 10
types of animals used in **103**.1, 5-6, 8, 22
unreliability of **103**.6
and veterinary research **103**.10
animal feed **87**.9, 11, 12-13, 27; **88**.35-6
animal rights **103**.32-3
animal rights activists
and animal experiments **103**.2, 9, 11
Government policies on **103**.23
laws against **103**.15-16
animal welfare **19**.24-40; **88**.32-3, 35-6; **90**.35
and abattoirs **19**.25, 26, 28
auction markets **19**.25-6, 34
European Union legislation on **19**.35, 36, 38, 39-40
and factory farming **19**.24, 30-1, 35-6, 37-8
and the 'five freedoms' **19**.24, 27-8, 32, 36
keeping animals healthy **19**.32-3, 36
and milk production **19**.17, 18, 30, 37
transportation of live animals **19**.25, 34-5, 36
UK legislation on **19**.24-5, 35, 36; **121**.7
and vegetarianism **19**.6, 24-40
welfare issues **19**.25
animals
and climate change **95**.3, 9, 11, 14-15
endangered species **95**.22
extinction of species **95**.1, 9, 14, 15, 26, 38
in the UK **95**.27
anorexia nervosa **84**.9; **123**.7, 33-4; **127**.1, 11-12
as auto-immune disease **127**.12
children and young people **127**.20
and self-harm **77**.10
anti-bullying practices
schools **122**.18, 25
workplaces **122**.39
anti-capitalism **98**.2
anti-depressant drugs **84**.35-6; **125**.24-5, 32
and adolescents **125**.8, 27
and children **123**.28; **125**.27

and ecstasy **114**.16
and postnatal depression **125**.18
and seasonal affective disorder **125**.38
and young people **123**.28
anti-doping initiatives **118**.25-8
international **118**.27-8, 31-2
UK **118**. 26-7, 28, 30
anti-obesity campaign, influence on children's body image **117**.22
anti-psychotic drugs **125**.19
anti-racism
and football **118**.14
laws see legislation and racism
anti-social driving habits **119**.9
anti-terrorism measures
and deportation **120**.38-9
and identity cards **120**.35
Muslims' views on **115**.34
antibiotics **88**.14
development of **105**.2
and farm livestock **19**.32
and medical research **103**.12
antiretroviral therapy (ART) **96**.36, 37, 38, 39
anxiety **84**.3, 9, 16-17
body dysmorphic disorder/dysmorphophobia **84**.16-17
and childhood depression **84**.29; **125**.28
dangers of severe **100**.21
defining **100**.21
and depression **100**.24
generalised anxiety disorder (GAD) **84**.3, 16
obsessive compulsive disorder (OCD) **84**.3, 9, 16
panic disorder **84**.16
phobias **84**.9, 16, 17
post-traumatic stress disorder (PTSD) **84**.9, 17
and stress **100**.2, 21
symptoms of **100**.21
trichotillomania **84**.17
and university students **84**.33
appetite-suppressing hormones **127**.38-9
apprenticeships **107**.36
aquifers, and global water supplies **76**.7, 16, 19
Arctic ice-cap melting **95**.3, 7, 8, 24, 33, 38
armed conflict
and the sexual exploitation of children **99**.20-1
war-affected children **99**.32-3
armed forces
and homosexuality **101**.25-6, 29, 32
recruitment age **120**.20
aromatherapy **81**.23, 36
and cancer **81**.10, 33
and multiple sclerosis **81**.30
and scientists **81**.28, 29
and stress relief **100**.37
arranged marriages **106**.15-18
arrests for drug use **114**.36
asbestos recycling **111**.35
asexual reproduction **90**.2, 20
Asian people
Asian-British women and body image **117**.29
British identity **115**.37
footballers **118**.13, 15-16

aspirations gap **107**.2
aspirin, toxicity levels compared to cannabis **80**.37
Assassins (eleventh-century Islamic terrorists) **92**.1, 6, 7
assault on children **120**.14-15
    in detention centres **120**.17
assertiveness training **117**.3
    and stress **100**.32
assessment, educational and gender equality **112**.11
assisted suicide
    defining **102**.1
    humanist view on **102**.1-2
    and the law **102**.5
        in Britain **102**.7, 8, 11, 15-16, 17, 20
        international comparisons **102**.7, 15
    public attitudes to **102**.9, 10, 17, 18, 27
    questions and answers on **102**.3-5
    and the right-to-die movement **102**.18-19
    safeguards **102**.2, 31
    'slippery slope' argument against **102**.2
    statistics **102**.17
    see also physician-assisted suicide (PAS)
asthma **91**.4
    increasing **119**.13, 26, 31
asylum seekers **120**.31
    in Britain *see* Britain, asylum seekers
    children **120**.21-2
    conditions for granting refugee status **89**.1
    fleeing from conflict **89**.7-8
    and HIV **96**.39
    and housing **85**.2, 13
    illegal immigration and identity cards **82**.2, 7, 8, 9, 10, 11
    numbers of **89**.2, 5, 6, 10
    top asylum nationalities **89**.1-2, 5, 6, 10
    top countries receiving **89**.2, 5, 10
atheism **94**.7, 15
Atkins diet **19**.15
    effect on eating habits **113**.14
ATM (Automatic Teller Machine) fraud **43**.27
attempted suicide
    consequences of **77**.35
    factors associated with **77**.1

    and homophobia **101**.22
    and the law **102**.4, 5
    and stress in young people **100**.4
    and subsequent suicide risk **77**.18
    support groups **77**.3
    and young men and women **77**.2, 5
attention deficit disorder (ADD) **127**.7
    and eating disorders **127**.10
attention deficit and hyperactivity disorder (ADHD)
    and eating disorders **127**.10
authoritarian parenting style **124**.8
authoritative parenting style **124**.8

B

babies
    food **87**.21
    and HIV **96**.31, 39
    killing of newborn **102**.25-6
    and poverty **110**.11
    weaning and iron in the diet **19**.5
backpackers
    global nomads **109**.10
    and insurance **109**.14-15
bacon, vegetarian **19**.21, 22
bacteria **88**.27, 28-9
balanced diet *see* healthy eating
banks
    basic bank accounts **74**.18, 24
    children and bank accounts **74**.6-7, 13
    current accounts **74**.18-19, 24
    financial education programmes for schools **74**.13
    Internet banking **74**.2, **104**.12
        and pharming **104**.33-4
        and phishing **104**.32-3
    and money management **106**.14
    overdrafts **74**.1, 18, 19, 21-2, 37
    savings accounts **74**.13, 19, 24
    and students **74**.2, 17, 21-2
    and young people **74**.9, 17-19

Volume numbers appear first (in bold) followed by page numbers; a change in volume number is preceded by a semi-colon.

Vol. **19** Looking at Vegetarianism
Vol. **20** Population Growth
Vol. **22** Confronting Child Abuse
Vol. **29** Gambling
Vol. **43** A Consumer Society
Vol. **60** Confronting Cancer
Vol. **69** The Media
Vol. **74** Money Matters
Vol. **75** Lone-Parent Families
Vol. **76** The Water Crisis
Vol. **77** Self-inflicted Violence
Vol. **78** Threatened Species
Vol. **79** Dealing with Homelessness
Vol. **80** The Cannabis Debate
Vol. **81** Alternative Therapies
Vol. **82** Protecting our Privacy
Vol. **83** Dealing with Crime
Vol. **84** Mental Wellbeing
Vol. **85** The Housing Crisis
Vol. **86** Smoking and your Health
Vol. **87** Genetic Modification

Vol. **88** Food and Nutrition
Vol. **89** Refugees
Vol. **90** Human and Animal Cloning
Vol. **91** Disability Issues
Vol. **92** Terrorism
Vol. **93** Binge Drinking
Vol. **94** Religions and Beliefs in Britain
Vol. **95** The Climate Crisis
Vol. **96** Preventing Sexual Diseases
Vol. **97** Energy Matters
Vol. **98** The Globalisation Issue
Vol. **99** Exploited Children
Vol. **100** Stress and Anxiety
Vol. **101** Sexuality and Discrimination
Vol. **102** The Ethics of Euthanasia
Vol. **103** Animal Rights
Vol. **104** Our Internet Society
Vol. **105** Ageing Issues
Vol. **106** Trends in Marriage
Vol. **107** Work Issues
Vol. **108** Domestic Violence

Vol. **109** Responsible Tourism
Vol. **110** Poverty
Vol. **111** The Waste Problem
Vol. **112** Women, Men and Equality
Vol. **113** Fitness and Health
Vol. **114** Drug Abuse
Vol. **115** Racial Discrimination
Vol. **116** Grief and Loss
Vol. **117** Self-Esteem and Body Image
Vol. **118** Focus on Sport
Vol. **119** Transport Trends
Vol. **120** The Human Rights Issue
Vol. **121** The Censorship Debate
Vol. **122** Bullying
Vol. **123** Young People and Health
Vol. **124** Parenting Issues
Vol. **125** Understanding Depression
Vol. **126** The Abortion Debate
Vol. **127** Eating Disorders

Basque separatists **92**.2, 19
batteries, recycling **111**.31, 35
beer drinking, young people **123**.1
begging
    children as beggars **99**.3, 4
    discouraging **79**.26, 34-5
    and yob-culture Britain **83**.5, 6
behaviour
    disorder symptoms in young people **84**.31
    gender differences **112**.28, 32-3, 35
    and healthy self-esteem **117**.30
    and low self-esteem **117**.5
    problems in schools **120**.16
    stress and behavioural changes **100**.33
    symptoms of workplace bullying **122**.31
benefits *see* state benefits
benefits of globalisation **98**.1, 12
benzene emissions, traffic **119**.15
bereavement **116**.1-18
    children *see* children and bereavement
    counselling **116**.6
    feelings **116**.1, 3-4, 5, 7-9, 10-11, 19, 21-2, 30
    help from GP **116**.2
    and homelessness **79**.2, 32
    and mental illness **84**.28
    and self-harm **77**.30
    and stress in young people **100**.2
    and suicide
        effects on families **77**.36-8
        survivors of **77**.39
    support **116**.2, 14-15
beta-blockers **118**.37
betting shops **29**.1, 3, 22, 40
    see also bookmakers; gambling
bigorexia **127**.19
bilateral trade agreements **98**.10
bill payments
    and direct debit **74**.9, 23
    and young people **74**.2, 23
binge drinking
    and advertising **93**.10-11
    and alcoholic poisoning **93**.29
    costs of **93**.1-2, 35
    and criminal/disorderly behaviour **93**.25
    defining **93**.10, 38
    getting help **93**.7
    health risks of **93**.4, 7
    and men **93**.1, 2, 36
    parents' worries about **124**.17
    public concern over **93**.5, 20
    statistics on **93**.35
    tips for cutting down **93**.34
    and women **93**.1, 10, 12, 18, 19-20
    and young people **93**.1, 6, 10, 12
binge eating **127**.2, 15-16
bingo **29**.2, 3, 7, 8, 9, 22
biodegradable plastics **111**.23
biodegradable waste **111**.3
biodiesel vehicles **119**.21
biodiversity
    and endangered animals **78**.6
    framework for measuring **78**.27
    and GM crops **87**.19, 30
    hot spots and population growth **20**.21
    loss of freshwater **76**.35
biodynamic massage **81**.1
bioenergy **87**.37; **97**.18
    biofuels **97**.9
    biomass **95**.34; **97**.5, 6, 9, 11, 18
biology and gender development **112**.28
biometrics **120**.33-4
biotechnology **87**.1, 3, 36
bipolar affective disorder (manic depression) **84**.3, 7, 8, 20; **125**.2, 4, 10, 19-20
    and cannabis **80**.14
    defining **125**.19
    and suicide **77**.17-18
    symptoms **84**.9; **125**.19
    treatments **84**.36; **125**.19-20
    and university students **84**.32, 33
    and violence **84**.18
birth control, teenagers **123**.22-3
    awareness of birth control services **123**.3
    see also contraception
birth country, non-white ethnic groups **115**.38
birth defects in cloned animals **90**.27, 28, 31, 34, 35, 39
birth rates
    births outside marriage **106**.4; **124**.22
    in developing countries **20**.1-2, 10, 38
    fall in **20**.4, 8, 16, 26, 36, 38; **106**.2
    and population ageing **20**.15
    to teenage mothers **75**.1
    see also teenage pregnancies
bisexuals **101**.1, 2, 4, 9, 11, 38
    issues facing young women **101**.19-20
    parents of **101**.17
'black on black' violence, and gun crime **83**.4
black people
    educational performance of children **115**.19-20
    pupils **115**.18-21
    women, body image **117**.29, 30
    and youth crime **83**.12
    see also employment and racism; ethnic minorities; racism
bladder cancer **60**.16, 17
blame, feelings of
    following bereavement **116**.8, 11, 19
    and low self-esteem **117**.6
blasphemy laws **94**.37, 39; **121**.16
    and cartoons of Mohammed **121**.12
blended families **124**.39
blood cholesterol levels **86**.10
    and exercise **113**.34
blood clots **86**.10
blood doping **118**.38
blood products, and HIV **96**.14
blood sugar levels **88**.15
    and binge eating **127**.15
boardroom positions, women **112**.18
body dysmorphic disorder/dysmorphophobia **84**.16-17; **127**.18-19
body image **117**.10-30

assessment of 117.18
boys 117.23
and eating disorders 127.27
and ethnicity 117.29-30
girls 117.19, 20-21, 22, 25
improving 117.10-11, 15, 18-19
and the media 117.11-12, 15, 17-18; 127.23, 25-6, 27
negative
 girls 117.25
 teenage girls 117.20-22
 women 117.14-15
positive 117.10
and self-esteem 117.10-11
study 127.29
women 117.19
 confidence about 112.31
 and ethnicity 117.29-30
 and media pressure 117.11-12, 14-15
 timeline 117.16-17
body language and avoiding bullying 122.5
body mass index (BMI) 88.8; 113.9, 11, 31; 127.32
measurement, children 127.36
body shapes 127.22
body weight 88.1, 12, 18
and exercise 113.34, 39
and smoking 86.25, 30, 35, 36
bombing attacks 92.9, 11
bonded labour 120.29
bone cancer 60.9, 11, 35
bone density, effects of eating disorders 127.5
bone marrow transplants 60.35, 36; 90.13
bookmakers 29.7, 9, 12, 36
see also betting shops; gambling; horse racing
border controls 89.20
borderline personality disorder (BPD) 77.11
borrowing, regional differences, UK 110.15
bottles
plastic 111.26-7
reusing 23
bowel cancer 60.3, 4, 6, 14, 16
boys and young men
academic performance 112.1, 8, 11

ambivalence towards girls 112.34
and body image 117.23
and cannabis use 80.2, 3, 11
and careers in childcare 112.23
and child labour 99.2
child soldiers 99.31, 36
and eating disorders 123.33
and education
 single-sex teaching 112.5-6
 underachievement 112.3
and gender equality 112.33-4
and Internet access 104.3
and non-traditional jobs 112.21
and the prevention of teenage pregnancies 75.23
and puberty 127.22
sexual behaviour 75.17, 18, 19, 20
sexual exploitation of 99.16, 21
street children 99.19
and suicide 77.1-2, 4, 17
 and anti-social behaviour 77.32-3
 and depression 77.32
 prevention 77.23
brain, effects of alcohol on 125.37
brain cancer 60.5
brain tumours in children 60.9, 10, 12
brands, and 'tweenagers' 69.11-12
breakfast, importance of 127.23
breakfast clubs 123.31
breast cancer 60.3, 4, 24-5
and age 60.23
and breast awareness 60.18, 22
and complementary therapies 81.23
and men 60.22
and radiotherapy 60.37
screening programme 60.13, 22, 23
and smoking 60.16
survival rates 60.4, 6, 13, 14, 27
treatment 60.4, 35
breast surgery, teenagers 117.26-8
breastfeeding
and teenage mothers 75.2
Britain, asylum seekers

Volume numbers appear first (in bold) followed by page numbers; a change in volume number is preceded by a semi-colon.

Vol. 19 Looking at Vegetarianism
Vol. 20 Population Growth
Vol. 22 Confronting Child Abuse
Vol. 29 Gambling
Vol. 43 A Consumer Society
Vol. 60 Confronting Cancer
Vol. 69 The Media
Vol. 74 Money Matters
Vol. 75 Lone-Parent Families
Vol. 76 The Water Crisis
Vol. 77 Self-inflicted Violence
Vol. 78 Threatened Species
Vol. 79 Dealing with Homelessness
Vol. 80 The Cannabis Debate
Vol. 81 Alternative Therapies
Vol. 82 Protecting our Privacy
Vol. 83 Dealing with Crime
Vol. 84 Mental Wellbeing
Vol. 85 The Housing Crisis
Vol. 86 Smoking and your Health
Vol. 87 Genetic Modification

Vol. 88 Food and Nutrition
Vol. 89 Refugees
Vol. 90 Human and Animal Cloning
Vol. 91 Disability Issues
Vol. 92 Terrorism
Vol. 93 Binge Drinking
Vol. 94 Religions and Beliefs in Britain
Vol. 95 The Climate Crisis
Vol. 96 Preventing Sexual Diseases
Vol. 97 Energy Matters
Vol. 98 The Globalisation Issue
Vol. 99 Exploited Children
Vol. 100 Stress and Anxiety
Vol. 101 Sexuality and Discrimination
Vol. 102 The Ethics of Euthanasia
Vol. 103 Animal Rights
Vol. 104 Our Internet Society
Vol. 105 Ageing Issues
Vol. 106 Trends in Marriage
Vol. 107 Work Issues
Vol. 108 Domestic Violence

Vol. 109 Responsible Tourism
Vol. 110 Poverty
Vol. 111 The Waste Problem
Vol. 112 Women, Men and Equality
Vol. 113 Fitness and Health
Vol. 114 Drug Abuse
Vol. 115 Racial Discrimination
Vol. 116 Grief and Loss
Vol. 117 Self-Esteem and Body Image
Vol. 118 Focus on Sport
Vol. 119 Transport Trends
Vol. 120 The Human Rights Issue
Vol. 121 The Censorship Debate
Vol. 122 Bullying
Vol. 123 Young People and Health
Vol. 124 Parenting Issues
Vol. 125 Understanding Depression
Vol. 126 The Abortion Debate
Vol. 127 Eating Disorders

appeals process **89**.13-14, 29, 33
asylum claims procedure **89**.12, 13-14
asylum legislation **89**.11, 12, 33, 39
citizenship acceptance **89**.37
costs of the asylum system **89**.11, 30
detention centres **89**.12, 13
health treatment **89**.19-20
legal aid **89**.29
number of asylum claims **89**.16, 18, 23
refused asylum applications **89**.11, 13-14, 18
welfare support **89**.12, 13, 14, 19, 30, 38
Britain, gender gap ranking **112**.29
Britain, poverty **110**.1-20
child poverty **110**.4, 5, 6-7
income inequality **110**.13, 14, 16
British identity
Asians **115**.37
and non-white ethnic groups **115**.38
British population
ethnic groups **115**.3
mixed-race relationships **115**.24
British tourists
and adventure travel **109**.9-10
and independent holidays **109**.8-9
brittle bone disease **91**.23
broadband services **104**.3
broadcasting regulation **121**.36-7
bronchitis **86**.9, 14
brownfield sites
and agricultural land **85**.28
decontaminating **85**.22
and new house-building **85**.9, 26, 34
and wildlife in London **85**.16-17
BSE (bovine spongiform encephalopathy)
and freedom of information **88**.14
and the transportation of live animals **19**.34, 35, 37
Buddhism **94**.6, 19, 21
abortion and contraception **126**.3
beliefs **94**.2, 4
and the Census (2001) **94**.3, 5, 28
festivals **94**.4
food rules **94**.10
funerals **116**.35
Golden Rule **94**.8, 11
and RE (religious education) **94**.9
budgeting
and lone parents **75**.38
and students **74**.2, 28, 30, 32
and young people **74**.2, 3, 14-15, 23
building access **91**.10-11, 14, 15-16
building industry, and energy efficiency **97**.36
building waste recycling **111**.35
bulimia nervosa **84**.9; **123**.7; **127**.1-2, 13-14
children and young people **127**.20
bullies
anger management training **122**.18
how to stop bullying **122**.2, 9-10
no-blame policy **122**.6-7
reasons for bullying **122**.8-9
bullying **22**.14; **91**.26; **122**.1-39
bullying behaviour **122**.8, 9-10, 15-16

cyberbullying **122**.19-26
definition **122**.1, 5, 8
extent of **122**.11, 17, 22-3
responding to bullying **122**.1-2, 5-6, 13, 16; **123**.3
cyberbullying **122**.19, 20, 21, 23, 24
workplace bullying **122**.27, 31-2, 33, 37-8
homophobic **101**.3, 13, 18, 19, 20, 21-2, 38-9
reasons for **122**.8-9
and self-harm **77**.6, 7, 9
and sexual harassment **112**.11
and stress in young people **100**.1, 2, 4
types of bullying **122**.15-116, 18
at work **122**.27-39
and workplace stress **100**.14, 15
young men and suicidal feelings **77**.32
and young people **122**.1-18
see also bullies; racist bullying; school bullying;
workplace bullying
burial **116**.37-9
alternative burials **116**.36, 38
on private land **116**.39
at sea **116**.39
bus travel
and pollution **119**.12
trends **119**.1
businesses and waste **111**.18

C

caffeine **114**.5; **118**.35
calcium **88**.6
teenagers' requirements **123**.6-7
call centres **98**.19-20
calorie intake **88**.1, 12
recording **113**.31
calorie restriction, and life expectancy **105**.29, 32
camera phones and bullying **122**.22-3, 26
campaigns
joining, and raising self-esteem **117**.33
litter **111**.8, 12
recycling **111**.25
waste prevention **111**.16
campylobacter **88**.28
cancer
and alcohol consumption **60**.1, 15; **93**.7, 8, 18, 28
bladder cancer **60**.16, 17
and blood cells **60**.34
bone cancer **60**.9, 11, 35
brain cancer **60**.5
and cannabis use **80**.10, 12, 13, 26
causes of **60**.1, 8
cells **60**.1, 33
cervical cancer **60**.5, 14, 16
childhood cancer **60**.8, 9-11, 13, 28, 32, 33-4
colorectal (bowel) cancer **60**.3, 4, 6, 14, 16
and complementary therapies **60**.39; **81**.3, 10, 21, 27, 32-3
and diet **19**.7, 15, 16; **60**.1-5, 14
early detection of **60**.36

and elderly people **60**.3, 7, 14
environmental factors in **60**.1, 2
and family history **60**.4, 5
inequalities in cancer incidence and mortality **60**.14
kidney cancer **60**.5, 9, 11, 16, 17
liver cancer **60**.5, 9, 16, 17
lymphomas **60**.4, 9, 10, 33
and meat consumption **19**.8, 15
melanoma (skin) cancer **60**.5, 18, 19-21
metastases **60**.1, 8
and milk consumption **19**.17
mouth, lips and throat cancer **60**.5, 15
multiple myeloma **60**.5
oesophageal cancer **60**.4, 15, 17
and older people **105**.3
pancreatic cancer **60**.4, 16, 17
prevention **60**.2, 3; **88**.17, 30
prostate cancer **105**.10
research **60**.2, 3
research and animal experiments **103**.8, 10, 13
and smoking **60**.1, 2, 3, 4, 13, 14, 15-17, 27; **86**.5,
    6, 9-11, 14-16, 31
stomach cancer **60**.4, 16, 17
and sunlight **60**.1, 2
support for people living with **60**.38
survival rates **60**.4, 5, 13, 27
symptoms **60**.1-2
    childhood cancers **60**.10, 11
testicular **60**.5, 11, 12, 13, 18, 26
thyroid cancer **60**.35
tumours **60**.1
and vegetarian diets **19**.19
womb **60**.5
see also breast cancer; lung cancer; prostate cancer
cancer salves (escharotics) **81**.33
cancer treatments **60**.1, 4, 5
and age of patients **60**.7, 14
biopsies **60**.33-4
and body scanning **60**.35, 36-7
bone marrow transplants **60**.35, 36
chemotherapy **60**.1, 4, 5, 26, 33, 34, 35, 36
childhood cancer **60**.9, 33-4

and early diagnosis **60**.7
effectiveness of **60**.7
hormone therapy **60**.4, 35, 36
and hospices **60**.8, 13
laser treatment **60**.35
nuclear medicine or isotope scanning **60**.37
painkillers **60**.7-8
radiotherapy **60**.1, 4, 5, 25, 33, 34, 35, 36
surgery **60**.1, 4, 5, 26, 33-4, 35
cannabinoids **118**.38
cannabis **114**.38
arguments against **80**.12
and the cannabis economy **80**.8-9, 18
cannabis oil **80**.1, 4, 6
cannabis resin **80**.1, 4, 6, 7
children's use **114**.20, 21
constituents of **80**.18
deaths **80**.16-17, 20
dependence on **80**.2, 12, 19, 21, 26
and driving **80**.2, 12, 13, 16, 17, 19, 21, 23; **114**.23
eating **80**.1, 4, 18, 20
and ecstasy **114**.16
effects of **80**.1-2; **114**.29
    on the brain **80**.13, 18
    on learning and educational performance **80**.19
facts and urban myths **80**.6-7
and hard drug use **80**.9-10, 29-30; 39
and health **80**.7, 10, 12, 13, 15
herbal cannabis (marijuana/grass) **80**.1, 4, 6, 11
home cultivation of **80**.32-3, 34
and the law **114**.38
legal position on **80**.23
legalisation debate **80**.4-6
medicinal use of **80**.5, 7, 12, 22, 34, 35-9; **114**.39
    Government policy on **80**.26, 34
    and home cultivation **80**.32
    and multiple sclerosis **80**.35
    as a painkiller **80**.22, 26, 37
and mental health **80**.7, 10, 12, 13, 14, 16, 19-20,
    26; **114**.37, 38
misconceptions **80**.9-10
and multiple sclerosis **81**.30, 31

Volume numbers appear first (in bold) followed by page numbers; a change in volume number is preceded by a semi-colon.

Vol. **19** Looking at Vegetarianism
Vol. **20** Population Growth
Vol. **22** Confronting Child Abuse
Vol. **29** Gambling
Vol. **43** A Consumer Society
Vol. **60** Confronting Cancer
Vol. **69** The Media
Vol. **74** Money Matters
Vol. **75** Lone-Parent Families
Vol. **76** The Water Crisis
Vol. **77** Self-inflicted Violence
Vol. **78** Threatened Species
Vol. **79** Dealing with Homelessness
Vol. **80** The Cannabis Debate
Vol. **81** Alternative Therapies
Vol. **82** Protecting our Privacy
Vol. **83** Dealing with Crime
Vol. **84** Mental Wellbeing
Vol. **85** The Housing Crisis
Vol. **86** Smoking and your Health
Vol. **87** Genetic Modification

Vol. **88** Food and Nutrition
Vol. **89** Refugees
Vol. **90** Human and Animal Cloning
Vol. **91** Disability Issues
Vol. **92** Terrorism
Vol. **93** Binge Drinking
Vol. **94** Religions and Beliefs in Britain
Vol. **95** The Climate Crisis
Vol. **96** Preventing Sexual Diseases
Vol. **97** Energy Matters
Vol. **98** The Globalisation Issue
Vol. **99** Exploited Children
Vol. **100** Stress and Anxiety
Vol. **101** Sexuality and Discrimination
Vol. **102** The Ethics of Euthanasia
Vol. **103** Animal Rights
Vol. **104** Our Internet Society
Vol. **105** Ageing Issues
Vol. **106** Trends in Marriage
Vol. **107** Work Issues
Vol. **108** Domestic Violence

Vol. **109** Responsible Tourism
Vol. **110** Poverty
Vol. **111** The Waste Problem
Vol. **112** Women, Men and Equality
Vol. **113** Fitness and Health
Vol. **114** Drug Abuse
Vol. **115** Racial Discrimination
Vol. **116** Grief and Loss
Vol. **117** Self-Esteem and Body Image
Vol. **118** Focus on Sport
Vol. **119** Transport Trends
Vol. **120** The Human Rights Issue
Vol. **121** The Censorship Debate
Vol. **122** Bullying
Vol. **123** Young People and Health
Vol. **124** Parenting Issues
Vol. **125** Understanding Depression
Vol. **126** The Abortion Debate
Vol. **127** Eating Disorders

names for **80**.4
potency of **80**.6, 11, 12, 20
prices **80**.6, 11
reclassification of **80**.7, 8, 14, 18, 20; **114**.37
    arguments for and against **80**.28
    government advertising on **80**.29-30
    public opinion on **80**.27-8
risks of **80**.2
sentences for cannabis possession **80**.23, 24, 30
side effects of **80**.2
smoking **80**.1, 2, 4
    health risks of **80**.7, 12, 13, 18-19
smuggling **114**.34
testing for **80**.2
THC content of **80**.2, 3, 4, 6-7, 11, 13, 15, 18, 19;
    114.37, 38
and the treatment demand indicator (TDI) **80**.3
users
    age of quitting **80**.13
    children **114**.20, 21
    and driving **80**.2, 12, 13, 16, 17, 19, 21
    lifetime prevalence **80**.3
    on negative effects of **80**.22
    on positive effects of **80**.21-2
    statistics on **80**.2, 3, 4, 6, 9, 18
what it looks like **80**.1, 4
where it comes from **80**.6
cans, recycling **111**.11, 23, 26, 31
capital flows **98**.5, 18
capitalism **98**.2
carbohydrates **88**.2, 5-6, 15
carbon
    carbon neutral societies/communities **95**.20, 29
    low carbon technologies **97**.4
    reducing exhaust emissions **95**.27
    and uncertainties about climate change **95**.7
carbon dioxide emissions **20**.23; **98**.14
    and air transport **97**.25
    and biomass **97**.18
    and energy efficiency **95**.30, 32, 38
    from fossil fuel burning **97**.1, 4
    from power stations **97**.3
    and global warming **95**.1, 2, 4, 5, 6, 9, 10
    levels in the atmosphere **95**.6, 10, 13, 19, 30
    public awareness of **97**.34
    reducing **95**.3, 5, 8, 14; **97**.2
    from transport **119**.14, 15, 16, 24, 30
    in the UK **97**.5, 21
    see also greenhouse gas
carbon monoxide **86**.4, 10, 14-15
    transport emissions **119**.15
cardboard recycling **111**.27, 31, 36
cardio-respiratory endurance **113**.24
care homes, older people in **105**.15
care leavers
    and homelessness **79**.4, 11, 18
    and teenage parenthood **75**.2
career advice **107**.32
    gender equality **112**.9, 21-2
career breaks **107**.27
career progression **107**.28

carers
    and flexible working **107**.17-18
    needs of carers **91**.7-8, 38
    and people with mental health problems **105**.39
carotenes **88**.2, 5
cars
    attitudes to car use **97**.35, 36
        male **112**.30
    car clubs **119**.33
    car jacking **83**.32
    cleaner fuels **119**.20-23
    congestion *see* congestion, traffic
    dependency on **119**.7
    drink-driving **93**.22, 30, 31, 35, 36, 37
    drugs and driving **114**.23-4
    and energy conservation **95**.5, 38
    fuel efficient **119**.20-24
    and greenhouse gases **95**.4
    morning-after motoring **93**.22
    ownership **119**.7, 11, 29
    recycling **111**.35
    reducing use of **119**.39
    sharing **119**.32-3
    speeding **119**.3, 4, 8
        and pedestrian injuries **119**.5, 30-31
        and speed cameras **119**.4, 17, 18
        speed limiters **119**.18
    tax and fuel efficiency **119**.24
    usage trends **119**.1, 7-9, 11, 13, 29
cartoons of Mohammed **121**.10-13, 15-16
cashless society **74**.9-11
casinos
    age restrictions **29**.18, 27
    lifting of restrictions on **29**.1, 2, 16, 17, 22
    online **29**.10-11, 12, 13
    and problem gamblers **29**.9
    and social class **29**.8
Catholic Church
    and abortion **126**.2, 36
    and assisted suicide **102**.15
    Catholic schools **94**.12-13, 30
    and contraception **20**.3; **126**.1-2
    tradition and beliefs **94**.2
    see also Christianity
cattle
    beef cattle **19**.31
    breeding **87**.1
    cloning **90**.30, 39
    dairy cows **19**.17, 18, 30, 37
    veal production **19**.30, 34, 37
CCTV (Closed Circuit Television) **82**.1, 6
    and crime prevention **82**.2, 3, 6
    and human rights **82**.24
    and RFID tags **82**.16
    statistics **82**.2
    and surveillance of public places **82**.3; **120**.33
    and workplace monitoring **82**.26, 27; **120**.32-3
celebrities
    and images of self-harm **77**.7, 14
    influence on girls' body image **117**.20-21
    as parental role models **124**.6

role models for boys **117**.23

smoking habits **86**.5, 6

cell culture **103**.14, 18, 19

cell differentiation **90**.11-12

cell division **90**.14

censorship **121**.1-2

films **121**.22, 23-5

and the Internet **121**.18-21

television **121**.36-7

and television violence **69**.9

cereals **88**.5-6, 15

cervical cancer **60**.5, 14, 16

CFCs (chlorofluorocarbons) **95**.1, 3, 4, 5

challenges as way of raising self-esteem **117**.33

challenging racism **115**.2

at work **115**.12

chat rooms

and bullying **122**.19-20, 21

and online child abuse **104**.25

and online safety **104**.20-1, 27, 35

use by children and young people **104**.5, 20-1

chemical/biological weapons, terrorist attacks using **92**.9, 31

chemicals recycling **111**.35

child abuse **22**.1-40; **120**.14-15

awareness of **22**.1

and care orders **22**.12

characteristics of abusers **22**.1, 4, 6

child protection registers **22**.1, 2, 11-12

dealing with suspected abuse **22**.8, 21

deaths **22**.2, 14, 17

effects of **22**.1, 4

emotional **22**.1-4, 7, 11-13

extent of **22**.10, 13-14

and 'false memory syndrome' **22**.3

and the law **22**.5

and low self-esteem **117**.7-8

neglect **22**.1, 2, 3, 4

and non-abusing family members **22**.21

online **104**.25

physical **22**.1, 2, 4, 7, 9, 12, 13, 27

and the police **22**.5, 17

reasons for **22**.2, 8

signs and symptoms of **22**.6, 7-8

and socio-economic background **22**.3, 13, 14

statistics **22**.1-2, 3, 4, 11-12

telling someone about the abuse **22**.4-5

see also sexual abuse

child labour **99**.1-15; **110**.39; **120**.18-20

and age of child **99**.2

attitudes to **99**.1

combating **99**.11-13

defining **99**.2, 3

demand for **99**.3

domestic work **99**.1, 4, 7-10

economic benefits of eliminating **99**.1, 6, 15

economic truths of **99**.14-15

and education **99**.3, 7, 10, 11-12, 15

and human rights **99**.4, 6

impact on a child **99**.2, 3

legislation and laws **99**.11

and poverty **99**.2, 3, 4, 11, 12, 14-15

reasons for **99**.1, 2-3, 3-4

statistics **99**.1, 2, 14

suitability for certain types of work **99**.4

and the tourist industry **109**.32

types of **99**.1, 2, 3, 4

child participation, and children's rights **120**.9-11

child pornography **22**.31-4, 37, 38, 40; **99**.1, 16, 17, 20, 24, 25

and the Internet **22**.31-2, 33

blocking access to sites **22**.38, 40

making it safer for children **22**.32

monitoring of sites **22**.33

as a 'victimless' offence **22**.34

child poverty **22**.30-1

global **110**.35, 36-7

and paedophiles **22**.30-1, 33

public awareness **110**.10

statistics **110**.7, 12

UK **110**.4, 5, 6-7, 10, 12, 13

child prostitution **99**.1, 16, 17, 25-6, 27-8

child protection **120**.14-15

abuses **110**.39

Volume numbers appear first (in bold) followed by page numbers; a change in volume number is preceded by a semi-colon.

Vol. **19** Looking at Vegetarianism

Vol. **20** Population Growth

Vol. **22** Confronting Child Abuse

Vol. **29** Gambling

Vol. **43** A Consumer Society

Vol. **60** Confronting Cancer

Vol. **69** The Media

Vol. **74** Money Matters

Vol. **75** Lone-Parent Families

Vol. **76** The Water Crisis

Vol. **77** Self-inflicted Violence

Vol. **78** Threatened Species

Vol. **79** Dealing with Homelessness

Vol. **80** The Cannabis Debate

Vol. **81** Alternative Therapies

Vol. **82** Protecting our Privacy

Vol. **83** Dealing with Crime

Vol. **84** Mental Wellbeing

Vol. **85** The Housing Crisis

Vol. **86** Smoking and your Health

Vol. **87** Genetic Modification

Vol. **88** Food and Nutrition

Vol. **89** Refugees

Vol. **90** Human and Animal Cloning

Vol. **91** Disability Issues

Vol. **92** Terrorism

Vol. **93** Binge Drinking

Vol. **94** Religions and Beliefs in Britain

Vol. **95** The Climate Crisis

Vol. **96** Preventing Sexual Diseases

Vol. **97** Energy Matters

Vol. **98** The Globalisation Issue

Vol. **99** Exploited Children

Vol. **100** Stress and Anxiety

Vol. **101** Sexuality and Discrimination

Vol. **102** The Ethics of Euthanasia

Vol. **103** Animal Rights

Vol. **104** Our Internet Society

Vol. **105** Ageing Issues

Vol. **106** Trends in Marriage

Vol. **107** Work Issues

Vol. **108** Domestic Violence

Vol. **109** Responsible Tourism

Vol. **110** Poverty

Vol. **111** The Waste Problem

Vol. **112** Women, Men and Equality

Vol. **113** Fitness and Health

Vol. **114** Drug Abuse

Vol. **115** Racial Discrimination

Vol. **116** Grief and Loss

Vol. **117** Self-Esteem and Body Image

Vol. **118** Focus on Sport

Vol. **119** Transport Trends

Vol. **120** The Human Rights Issue

Vol. **121** The Censorship Debate

Vol. **122** Bullying

Vol. **123** Young People and Health

Vol. **124** Parenting Issues

Vol. **125** Understanding Depression

Vol. **126** The Abortion Debate

Vol. **127** Eating Disorders

registers **22**.1, 2, 11-12

child safety concerns of parents **124**.13-14

child sex tourism **109**.32, 35-6
  awareness of **109**.36
  legal framework **109**.35-6

child soldiers **99**.1, 4, 29-39; **120**.20
  age of **99**.29-30
  benefits of ending child soldier use **99**.39
  defining **99**.29
  girls **99**.29, 31, 36
  harmful effects of being **99**.31, 36
  and human rights atrocities **99**.30
  and non-governmental armed groups **99**.30
  statistics **99**.29

child tax credit (CTC) **110**.6, 7

childbirth
  deaths in **112**.39
  see also post-natal depression

childcare
  careers, men **112**.23-4
  costs **124**.3
  emergency childcare **107**.22
  and fathers **124**.7-10, 11
  and flexible working **107**.12, 16, 21, 23
  and grandmothers **124**.37-8
  and lone parents **75**.30, 38, 39
  and teenage mothers **75**.10
  underprovision **110**.6-7

childhood problems as cause of low self-esteem **117**.7-8, 31, 32-3

childhood obesity **88**.3, 11; **113**.1-5, 6, 7-8, 12; **127**.33, 36-7

childless people **20**.26

childlessness for financial reasons **124**.18

childminders
  and the smacking of children **22**.22, 23-4
  and smoking **22**.22, 23

children
  and advertising **43**.6, 7, 8, 9; **69**.11-13, 14
  age and children's rights **120**.5
  alcohol and mental health problems **125**.9
  of alcoholics **93**.30
  and Attention Deficit Hyperactivity Disorder (ADHD) **84**.5, 29
  and bereavement **116**.1, 9, 19-28
    bereavement statistics **116**.20, 21
    bereavement support **116**.15, 28
  and body image **117**.14, 19, 22, 25
  cancer in childhood **60**.8, 9-11, 13, 28, 32, 33-4
  and censorship
    films **121**.23-5
    video games **121**.32-3
    videos **121**.26
  childhood leukaemia and medical research **103**.12
  of cohabiting couples **106**.21-2; **124**.22
  commercial pressure on **43**.6-8
  and compulsive gambling **29**.19, 25
  costs of raising **124**.3
  cycling **119**.28, 30
  death
    children's questions about **116**.26-7
    children's understanding of **116**.22
  deaths of
    child abuse **22**.2, 14, 17
    mortality rates **20**.36, 40
    murders **22**.30, 31
    and poverty **110**.35
  and depression **123**.27-8; **125**.27-8
  in developing countries
    deaths and diseases from water-related illness **76**.2, 3, 5, 9, 13, 14
    and global water supplies **76**.13-14
    and hygiene education **76**.14
    and sanitation provision **76**.13-14
    and water collection **76**.13, 19-20
  developing responsibility **124**.13-14
  diet **113**.4-5
  disciplining and physical punishment of **22**.22, 23-7
  and divorce **106**.27, 33-8; **124**.24, 29-30, 32-4
  and domestic violence
    blaming themselves **108**.20
    coping strategies **108**.23
    effects of **108**.11, 28
    and keeping women at home **108**.15
    living with abuse **108**.26, 27
    loss of confidence **108**.20
    and neglect **108**.20
    seeking professional help **108**.23, 28, 36
  and drug use **114**.20-22, 25
  of drug users **114**.28
  drugs testing at school **114**.26
  and eating disorders **127**.3, 20-21
  ethnic minorities, and education **115**.18, 19-21
  exercise, lack of **113**.1, 7, 8
  explaining suicide to young children **77**.37
  falling out with parents **124**.18
  and fathers **124**.7-11
  and food advertising **88**.10, 11, 20, 35, 37
  and food in school **123**.32
  and funerals **116**.23, 26
  gender development **112**.35
  and grief **116**.19-28
  health, and transport **119**.13-14, 31
  and HIV/AIDS **96**.20, 39
  homeless **79**.4, 8
  inactivity **113**.1, 7, 8
  and the Internet **104**.3-5, 9-11, 13, 17-29
  of lone parents **75**.28, 29, 39; **124**.33-4
  and media violence **121**.33, 34, 35
  and mental health problems **125**.16
  and mental illness **84**.1, 5-6
  and mobile phone tracking **82**.19, 20
  and money matters **74**.6-7, 12-13
  needs **120**.2
  obesity *see* childhood obesity
  and passive smoking **60**.17
  in prison (under 18s) **83**.23, 27-9
  and poverty *see* child poverty
  and racism **115**.1-2, 9
  refugees **89**.39; **120**.21-2
  relationships with separated fathers **75**.36
  and road accidents **119**.5, 28, 30-31

and road safety **119**.5-6
safety concerns of parents **124**.13-14
smacking **22**.22, 23-4, 26
and smoking **86**.1, 8, 14-15, 24-5, 26; **123**.11-13
and stepfamilies **124**.23-8
and suicide **123**.35
and sun exposure **60**.19, 20-1
of teenage mothers **75**.2, 7-8
and television
    and the 9 p.m. watershed **69**.10
    advertising **69**.11-13
    children's programmes **69**.3, 5, 6
    parental control of viewing **121**.26, 27, 34
    programme content regulation **69**.2, 10
    protection of children **69**.3
time spent with parents **106**.2
    fathers **124**.7-8, 9, 11
travel to school **119**.26, 29-30
and vegetarian diets **19**.1
and video classification **121**.32-3
and video games **121**.32-3
children's rights **120**.1-22
and age of children **120**.1, 2
and child abuse **120**.14-15
and children's needs **120**.2
and justice system **120**.1-2, 12-13
and participation in decision-making **120**.9-11
denied by poverty **110**.36-7
refugees **120**.21-2
and responsibilities **120**.1
timeline **120**.3
to vote **120**.7-8
in the UK **120**.2
UN Convention on the Rights of the Child **120**.4-6
Chinese medicine **81**.2, 3
and cancer **81**.33
and endangered species **81**.15
herbal medicine **81**.14-15, 39
see also complementary medicine (CM)
chip cards **43**.34-5
chiropractic **81**.8-9, 23, 36
effectiveness of **81**.24

misdiagnosis and dangers of **81**.23, 24
regulation of **81**.23
and scientists **81**.28, 29
chlamydia **75**.16, 17; **96**.2-3, 4, 9; **123**.26
and HIV **96**.12
increase in cases of **96**.8, 10
signs and symptoms **96**.5
testing for **96**.2, 3, 5
treatment **96**.5
chocolate **88**.18-19, 31
cholera **76**.2, 12, 13, 32
cholesterol
and coronary heart disease **19**.10, 19
and exercise **113**.34
and smoking **86**.10
and vegetarian diets **19**.15, 20
Christianity
and abortion and contraception **126**.1-2
beliefs **94**.1-2, 3
and the Census (2001) **94**.3, 5, 6, 28
and church attendance **94**.5, 6
and faith **94**.39
festivals **94**.3
funerals **116**.33
Golden Rule **94**.8, 11
and homosexuality **101**.5-7
and 'honour killings' **94**.30
and images of self-harm **77**.7
new religious movements/cults **94**.19, 21, 25
and RE (religious education) **94**.9, 15
and young people **94**.6-7
chromosomes **87**.2, 22
Church of England **94**.1, 3
and abortion and contraception **126**.1
disestablishment **94**.37
and marriage **106**.9-10
and RE (religious education) **94**.15, 31
schools **94**.12-14, 30
chymosin **87**.13
cigarettes **114**.5
and cannabis users **80**.26
chemicals in **86**.4, 9-10

Volume numbers appear first (in bold) followed by page numbers; a change in volume number is preceded by a semi-colon.

Vol. **19** Looking at Vegetarianism
Vol. **20** Population Growth
Vol. **22** Confronting Child Abuse
Vol. **29** Gambling
Vol. **43** A Consumer Society
Vol. **60** Confronting Cancer
Vol. **69** The Media
Vol. **74** Money Matters
Vol. **75** Lone-Parent Families
Vol. **76** The Water Crisis
Vol. **77** Self-inflicted Violence
Vol. **78** Threatened Species
Vol. **79** Dealing with Homelessness
Vol. **80** The Cannabis Debate
Vol. **81** Alternative Therapies
Vol. **82** Protecting our Privacy
Vol. **83** Dealing with Crime
Vol. **84** Mental Wellbeing
Vol. **85** The Housing Crisis
Vol. **86** Smoking and your Health
Vol. **87** Genetic Modification

Vol. **88** Food and Nutrition
Vol. **89** Refugees
Vol. **90** Human and Animal Cloning
Vol. **91** Disability Issues
Vol. **92** Terrorism
Vol. **93** Binge Drinking
Vol. **94** Religions and Beliefs in Britain
Vol. **95** The Climate Crisis
Vol. **96** Preventing Sexual Diseases
Vol. **97** Energy Matters
Vol. **98** The Globalisation Issue
Vol. **99** Exploited Children
Vol. **100** Stress and Anxiety
Vol. **101** Sexuality and Discrimination
Vol. **102** The Ethics of Euthanasia
Vol. **103** Animal Rights
Vol. **104** Our Internet Society
Vol. **105** Ageing Issues
Vol. **106** Trends in Marriage
Vol. **107** Work Issues
Vol. **108** Domestic Violence

Vol. **109** Responsible Tourism
Vol. **110** Poverty
Vol. **111** The Waste Problem
Vol. **112** Women, Men and Equality
Vol. **113** Fitness and Health
Vol. **114** Drug Abuse
Vol. **115** Racial Discrimination
Vol. **116** Grief and Loss
Vol. **117** Self-Esteem and Body Image
Vol. **118** Focus on Sport
Vol. **119** Transport Trends
Vol. **120** The Human Rights Issue
Vol. **121** The Censorship Debate
Vol. **122** Bullying
Vol. **123** Young People and Health
Vol. **124** Parenting Issues
Vol. **125** Understanding Depression
Vol. **126** The Abortion Debate
Vol. **127** Eating Disorders

deaths caused by **80**.10
  herbal **86**.37
  low tar **86**.32
circulatory diseases **86**.9, 10
cities *see* cars, congestion; urban areas; urban growth
citizenship **89**.37
Citizenship Education in schools **108**.25
civil liberties
  and drugs legalisation **114**.39
   cannabis **80**.5
Civil Partnerships **101**.9, 10, 23, 29, 32, 33-5
civil protest **121**.14
civil wars **89**.7-8
class *see* social class
class A drugs
  increasing use **114**.14
  prices **114**.6-7
  young people's use **114**.21
classification
  of drugs **114**.1, 31, 32
  of films **121**.22, 23-5, 29-30
  of video games **121**.32-3
claustrophobia **84**.16, 17
cleaner fuels **119**.20-23
clenbuterol hydrochloride **118**.35
climate change
  abrupt **95**.17-20
  dangerous **95**.12
  deaths attributed to **95**.11, 23, 25, 38, 39
  economic costs of **95**.25
  effects of **95**.11-28
  and global water supplies **76**.1, 3, 5, 8
  information on **95**.1-10
  misconceptions **95**.3
  and nuclear power **97**.19-20, 21, 22
  and oil production **95**.16-17
  positive and negative feedbacks **95**.8, 10, 15
  public awareness of factors contributing to **97**.34
  reasons for **95**.2, 9
  and renewable energy sources
   bioenergy **97**.18
   case for **97**.1-2
   and wind energy **97**.15
  and social justice **95**.16, 17
  solutions **95**.29-39
  and species extinction **78**.10, 11
  and transport emissions **119**.14, 30
  in the UK **95**.3, 5, 15, 17
  and water management **76**.34
  see also energy efficiency; global warming; greenhouse
   gas emissions
cloning *see* animal cloning; human reproductive cloning;
  therapeutic cloning
clubs **86**.17, 19, 20-3; **91**.17
  and binge drinking **93**.1, 2
  to pay cost of policing drunks **93**.21, 35, 36
co-education, effect on girls **112**.6
co-parenting after divorce **124**.32
coastal areas
  development and population growth **20**.14, 22, 24
  flooding and climate change **95**.2, 3, 5, 7, 9, 11, 14, 15

cocaine **114**.5, 10
  mixed with other drugs **114**.16
  prevalence of use **114**.14
  prices **114**.7
  smuggling **114**.34
  use by young people **80**.2
  see also crack cocaine
cocoa industry and child labour **120**.19
coffee growers **98**.13, 17
  poverty due to trade rules **110**.22
Cognitive Behaviour Therapy (CBT) **29**.29-30; **84**.35
  for bulimia nervosa (CBT-BN) **127**.14
  and Seasonal Affective Disorder **125**.38
cohabitation
  age at first **106**.10
  changing views on **106**.4
  and stability for children **124**.22
  and 'common law' marriages **106**.8
  legal protection for cohabitees **106**.7-8, 10
  and likelihood of marriage **106**.5
  reasons for **106**.11
  and splitting up **106**.21
  statistics **20**.26
colorectal (bowel) cancer **60**.3, 4, 6, 14, 16
colour as grounds for discrimination **115**.7
commercialisation in sport **118**.9
commodity prices **98**.10, 17
'common law' marriages **106**.8, 9-10
communication
  and abortion **126**.11
  importance in bereavement **116**.24-5
  importance in depression **125**.3, 39
   young people **125**.8
  and eating disorders **127**.30
  and self-esteem **117**.4
communications data **82**.5, 33-4
  government monitoring of **82**.1-2
  and the law **82**.33-4
communities
  and identity cards **82**.11
  sustainable **85**.32, 38, 39
community sentences **83**.34
  and young offenders **83**.13, 16, 24-5, 30
community-based tourism **109**.19, 27, 33-4, 38
compassion, and euthanasia **102**.12-13, 30
compensation orders **83**.24, 34
competitive sport in schools **118**.4
complaints
  about children and advertising **43**.9
  about goods and services **43**.22
  rise in consumer **43**.19
  sex discrimination **112**.14
  sources of help **43**.22-3
complementary medicine (CM)
  and cancer **60**.39
  and consumer choice **81**.37
  and consumer ignorance **81**.35
  defining **81**.1, 4
  and depression **125**.39
   manic depression **125**.20
  and diagnosis **81**.34

disciplines within **81**.1-3
effectiveness of **81**.22-4, 26, 27, 31
expenditure on **81**.23, 37, 39
and GPs **81**.21
and misdiagnosis **81**.23
and multiple sclerosis **81**.30-1
and the placebo effect **81**.26, 28, 34
regulation of **81**.23
safety of **81**.27, 31
and scientists **81**.28-9
and self-care **81**.36-7
complex carbohydrates **88**.2
compost **111**.3
composting waste **111**.6, 23, 31, 33
compulsive eating **127**.20-21
compulsive exercise **113**.37-8
compulsive gambling **29**.18-40
abstinence or control **29**.30, 31
advice on controlling **29**.20, 39-40
asking questions about **29**.25, 30, 31-3
and betting games **29**.35
and children **29**.19, 25
consequences of **29**.27-8
defining **29**.31, 39
families and what to do **29**.28
and fruit machines **29**.35, 36
and Gamblers Anonymous **29**.15, 18, 19, 25, 26, 31-3
and the National Lottery **29**.9, 19, 21, 26
online **29**.14, 19
overcoming **29**.29-30
and personality traits **29**.32-3, 39
prevalence of **29**.1-2
reasons for addiction **29**.27
relapse-prevention strategy **29**.30
signs and symptoms of **29**.24-5, 27, 29-30
and UK gambling law reforms **29**.16, 17, 18-19, 22-3
and willpower **29**.31-2
and young people **29**.2, 19, 37-8
compulsory admission for eating disorders **127**.29
computer games
and boys' underachievement **112**.3
violence, influence on children **121**.32-3, 35

computer research, in medicine **103**.13-14, 17, 19, 22
computers
and academic achievement **112**.3
home computer use **43**.2
and older people **105**.5
personal computer ownership **69**.1, 2
see also Internet
conception **123**.22
rate, young people **126**.30-31
condoms **75**.15, 16, 17, 22; **101**.3-4; **123**.23
availability of **96**.2
and HIV **96**.12, 14, 16, 24, 25, 29, 30, 32, 33, 34
and the prevention of STIs **96**.1-2, 9; **123**.24, 25
and sex education **75**.22
and teenage sex **75**.17
confidentiality
and abortion **126**.13, 28, 29
effect on teenage conception rate **126**.30
and eating disorders **127**.28
Confucianism **94**.11
congestion, traffic **119**.11
congestion charging **119**.12, 34-5, 38
rail **119**.35
and road building **119**.12
conservation
animal species **78**.11
and the exotic pet trade **78**.21-2
plant species **78**.17
tree species **78**.12
zoo conservation **78**.24-5
see also endangered species; extinction
construction industry, recruitment of women **112**.25
consumer awareness **43**.14-40
consumer rights **43**.16-18
buying goods **43**.16
buying a service **43**.18
consumer safety **43**.18
and extended warranties **43**.20-1
faulty goods **43**.16-17
limits to **43**.25
private sales and auctions **43**.17-18, 25
and safety **43**.18

Volume numbers appear first (in bold) followed by page numbers; a change in volume number is preceded by a semi-colon.

Vol. **19** Looking at Vegetarianism
Vol. **20** Population Growth
Vol. **22** Confronting Child Abuse
Vol. **29** Gambling
Vol. **43** A Consumer Society
Vol. **60** Confronting Cancer
Vol. **69** The Media
Vol. **74** Money Matters
Vol. **75** Lone-Parent Families
Vol. **76** The Water Crisis
Vol. **77** Self-inflicted Violence
Vol. **78** Threatened Species
Vol. **79** Dealing with Homelessness
Vol. **80** The Cannabis Debate
Vol. **81** Alternative Therapies
Vol. **82** Protecting our Privacy
Vol. **83** Dealing with Crime
Vol. **84** Mental Wellbeing
Vol. **85** The Housing Crisis
Vol. **86** Smoking and your Health
Vol. **87** Genetic Modification

Vol. **88** Food and Nutrition
Vol. **89** Refugees
Vol. **90** Human and Animal Cloning
Vol. **91** Disability Issues
Vol. **92** Terrorism
Vol. **93** Binge Drinking
Vol. **94** Religions and Beliefs in Britain
Vol. **95** The Climate Crisis
Vol. **96** Preventing Sexual Diseases
Vol. **97** Energy Matters
Vol. **98** The Globalisation Issue
Vol. **99** Exploited Children
Vol. **100** Stress and Anxiety
Vol. **101** Sexuality and Discrimination
Vol. **102** The Ethics of Euthanasia
Vol. **103** Animal Rights
Vol. **104** Our Internet Society
Vol. **105** Ageing Issues
Vol. **106** Trends in Marriage
Vol. **107** Work Issues
Vol. **108** Domestic Violence

Vol. **109** Responsible Tourism
Vol. **110** Poverty
Vol. **111** The Waste Problem
Vol. **112** Women, Men and Equality
Vol. **113** Fitness and Health
Vol. **114** Drug Abuse
Vol. **115** Racial Discrimination
Vol. **116** Grief and Loss
Vol. **117** Self-Esteem and Body Image
Vol. **118** Focus on Sport
Vol. **119** Transport Trends
Vol. **120** The Human Rights Issue
Vol. **121** The Censorship Debate
Vol. **122** Bullying
Vol. **123** Young People and Health
Vol. **124** Parenting Issues
Vol. **125** Understanding Depression
Vol. **126** The Abortion Debate
Vol. **127** Eating Disorders

secondhand goods **43**.25

unfair contract terms **43**.18

consumer spending

boycotts **43**.4

and children **43**.6-8

expenditure patterns **43**.1, 2, 3-4

gap between rich and poor **43**.13

and globalisation **43**.10-11

insights into consumer markets **43**.3-4

see also shopping

consumer terrorism **92**.11

consumerism and relative poverty **110**.22-3

consumers

awareness surveys **43**.14, 15-16

and cannabis economy **80**.8-9

and child labour **99**.12

complaints **43**.9, 19, 22-3

and RFID tags **82**.16-17, 35

consumption

and population growth **20**.8, 22-3, 24

contraception **75**.15-16; **123**.22-3

advice **126**.23-4

'double dutch' method of **96**.2

emergency contraception (EC) **75**.3, 13, 15-16, 17; **126**.24

and family planning services **75**.16

and the male pill **20**.38-9

and men **96**.13

and microbicides **96**.34

and population growth **20**.3

religious views **126**.1-3

sterilisation **75**.15, 16

vasectomies **75**.16

and young people **75**.2-3, 13; **123**.22-3

under 16s **75**.4, 9

see also condoms; family planning; pill, contraceptive

contract sales **107**.22

controlling behaviour **108**.2, 15, 19

coral reefs, and climate change **95**.11, 13

coral trade **78**.21

coroner **116**.32

corporal punishment

and children's rights **120**.15

corporate accountability **98**.27

corporate globalisation **98**.25-7

corporate lobbying **98**.4

corporate responsibility **98**.6, 26, 29, 37-8

cosmetic testing on animals **103**.23

cosmetic surgery **117**.21, 24-5

and ethnicity **117**.29-30

costs

of abortion **126**.12

of the asylum system **89**.11, 30

of cleaner vehicles **119**.20-24

of domestic violence **108**.10

of education, developing countries **110**.38

of gym membership **113**.36

of identity cards **120**.35-6

of litter clearing **111**.8

of mental health problems **125**.16

of motoring **119**.14

of obesity **127**.33-4, 37

of poverty elimination **110**.23

of psychological therapy **125**.7

of raising a child **124**.3

as reason for smaller families **124**.18

of smoking **86**.7, 25, 33

to health service of coronary heart disease **113**.20

of waste **111**.18

cot death **86**.25

cotinine **86**.13

cotton **87**.25, 29, 30, 31, 38; **98**.24

council tax **91**.3

and pensioners **110**.19

counselling

for childhood bullying **122**.6

for depression **125**.30-31

eating disorders **127**.21, 29

and help with stress **100**.32, 34

and mental illness **84**.10

for post-natal depression **125**.18

students and counselling services **84**.32, 33

and testing for HIV **96**.1

and voluntary euthanasia **102**.2

and young people **84**.24, 31-2

counter-terrorism **92**.13

aviation security **92**.32, 34

contingency planning and resilience **92**.33

counter-terrorist measures in London **92**.31-2

and Islam **92**.26, 28-9

public attitudes to **92**.35

security measures **92**.38

targeting terrorist funds **92**.22

White convictions in the UK **92**.27-8

counterfeit fraud **43**.26

countryside, and the production and use of energy **97**.24-5

courts of law

children's access to **120**.1-2

and debts **74**.35

and the media **69**.38

and torture evidence **120**.39

crack cocaine **114**.10

increasing usage **114**.14

prices **114**.7

see also cocaine

cranial osteopathy **81**.2

creativity, and emotional health and wellbeing **84**.24, 27

credit

advantages and disadvantages of **74**.23

bank overdrafts **74**.1, 18, 19, 21-2

buying on **43**.29, 31

cancelling a credit agreement **43**.32

credit ratings **74**.25, 27

extra protection when using **43**.32

interest rates **74**.23

obtaining **74**.23

reference agencies **43**.31-2

settling up early **43**.32-3

and students **74**.30

see also debt

credit cards **74**.26-7

card-not-present fraud **43**.26
and the cashless society **74**.9-11
chip cards **43**.34-5
credit reference agencies **74**.25, 27
and e-shopping **104**.5, 6
fraud **43**.26-7, 28
interest rates **43**.28; **74**.26, 27
limits **74**.26
minimum repayments **74**.26
'payment holidays' **74**.26
shopping around for **74**.25-6
store cards **74**.27
and students **74**.3, 30, 32, 36, 37
theft, and RFID tags **82**.16
and under 18s **43**.23-4
use of **43**.28
and young people **74**.15, 16, 23
cremation **116**.37-8
crime
alcohol-related **93**.1, 5, 20, 25
and anti-social behaviour **79**.26
and children of lone parents **75**.29
and divorce **106**.31
and drug abuse **80**.28
and drug users **114**.12
fear of **83**.6
and gambling **29**.1, 17, 22
hate crime **101**.29, 36-7
and identity cards
forging **82**.7, 8
as a means of combating crime **82**.7, 8, 10, 11
and mental illness **84**.4
racially motivated **115**.9-10
rates **83**.1-2, 3, 13, 14
religiously motivated **115**.27
and RFID cards **82**.17
statistics **83**.1-2, 3, 6
and surveillance **82**.17-18
and teenage parenthood **75**.2
terrorism and organised crime **92**.22
victims of **83**.6, 7, 14
waste dumping **111**.20

wildlife **78**.19, 38-9
and yob-culture Britain **83**.5-6
see also fraud; victims of crime; violent crime; young
offenders
crime prevention **83**.31-9
car jacking **83**.32
and CCTV **82**.2, 3, 6
and the Internet
child protection **104**.28-9
pharming **104**.33-4
phishing **104**.32-3
personal safety **83**.31-2
and the police **83**.32
and restorative justice **83**.37-8
and young offenders **83**.35-6
and youth justice **83**.33
crime and young people **83**.11-30
and alcohol abuse **83**.15, 35-6
attitudes to reporting crime **83**.17
and bullying **83**.11
crime committed **83**.14-15
and crime prevention **83**.35-6
and drugs **83**.12, 17
and fear of crime **83**.16, 17, 18
and gang culture **83**.11-12
and personal experience of crime **83**.16-17, 18
rates of juvenile crime **83**.13
reoffending rates **83**.13
statistics **83**.14-16
under-16s' experience of and attitudes to **83**.16-17
as victims of crime **83**.7, 14
criminal justice system
and children's rights **120**.12
costs of domestic violence to **108**.10
and restorative justice **83**.37-8
criminal responsibility, age of **83**.29-30
criminality
and high self-esteem **117**.7
and mental health problems **125**.16
crop biotechnology *see* genetically modified (GM) crops
crop rotation **87**.8, 19, 24; **88**.14
crop yields **87**.25, 29

Volume numbers appear first (in bold) followed by page numbers; a change in volume number is preceded by a semi-colon.

Vol. **19** Looking at Vegetarianism
Vol. **20** Population Growth
Vol. **22** Confronting Child Abuse
Vol. **29** Gambling
Vol. **43** A Consumer Society
Vol. **60** Confronting Cancer
Vol. **69** The Media
Vol. **74** Money Matters
Vol. **75** Lone-Parent Families
Vol. **76** The Water Crisis
Vol. **77** Self-inflicted Violence
Vol. **78** Threatened Species
Vol. **79** Dealing with Homelessness
Vol. **80** The Cannabis Debate
Vol. **81** Alternative Therapies
Vol. **82** Protecting our Privacy
Vol. **83** Dealing with Crime
Vol. **84** Mental Wellbeing
Vol. **85** The Housing Crisis
Vol. **86** Smoking and your Health
Vol. **87** Genetic Modification

Vol. **88** Food and Nutrition
Vol. **89** Refugees
Vol. **90** Human and Animal Cloning
Vol. **91** Disability Issues
Vol. **92** Terrorism
Vol. **93** Binge Drinking
Vol. **94** Religions and Beliefs in Britain
Vol. **95** The Climate Crisis
Vol. **96** Preventing Sexual Diseases
Vol. **97** Energy Matters
Vol. **98** The Globalisation Issue
Vol. **99** Exploited Children
Vol. **100** Stress and Anxiety
Vol. **101** Sexuality and Discrimination
Vol. **102** The Ethics of Euthanasia
Vol. **103** Animal Rights
Vol. **104** Our Internet Society
Vol. **105** Ageing Issues
Vol. **106** Trends in Marriage
Vol. **107** Work Issues
Vol. **108** Domestic Violence

Vol. **109** Responsible Tourism
Vol. **110** Poverty
Vol. **111** The Waste Problem
Vol. **112** Women, Men and Equality
Vol. **113** Fitness and Health
Vol. **114** Drug Abuse
Vol. **115** Racial Discrimination
Vol. **116** Grief and Loss
Vol. **117** Self-Esteem and Body Image
Vol. **118** Focus on Sport
Vol. **119** Transport Trends
Vol. **120** The Human Rights Issue
Vol. **121** The Censorship Debate
Vol. **122** Bullying
Vol. **123** Young People and Health
Vol. **124** Parenting Issues
Vol. **125** Understanding Depression
Vol. **126** The Abortion Debate
Vol. **127** Eating Disorders

cross training **113**.28
crystal healing **81**.2
cults *see* NRMs (New Religious Movements)
cultural differences and mixed-faith relationships **115**.39
cultural traditions and children's rights **120**.2
culture and religion **126**.1
curfew orders **83**.25, 30, 34
currency speculation **98**.38
current account balances, regional differences **110**.15
curriculum, schools, gender equality **112**.9
Cushing's syndrome and depression **125**.5
cyberbullying **122**.19-26
cycling **119**.25, 29
    children **119**.28; **124**.14
    health benefits **119**.39
    helmets **119**.28
    to school **119**.30

D

D notice **121**.37
D&E (surgical dilation and evacuation) **126**.10, 14
dairy foods **88**.6, 15
dangerous and severe personality disorder (DSPD), and
    the draft mental health bill **84**.36-7
data protection
    communications data **82**.33-4
    and RFID tags **82**.16
    and self-regulation **82**.5
Data Protection Acts **82**.21-2, 37-8, 39
DBD (disruptive behaviour disorder) influence of media
    violence **121**.35
deaths **20**.25, 27, 30
    abortion-related **20**.25, 27, 30
    AIDS, impact on children **110**.37
    alcohol-related **93**.8-9, 11, 18, 31, 35, 37
    cancer **60**.3, 7, 27; **81**.23, 32
        and hospices **60**.8
        lung cancer **60**.3, 15, 27
        skin cancer **60**.19
        and smoking **60**.15, 27
    of children
        child abuse **22**.2, 14, 17
        cyclists **119**.28
    mortality rates **20**.36, 40
        murders **22**.30, 31
     pedestrians **119**.5, 30
     and poverty **110**.35
    children's questions about death **116**.26-7
    children's understanding of death **116**.22
    and drug misuse **80**.10, 11; **114**.12, 13
        cannabis **80**.16-17, 20
    ex-prisoners **114**.14
    excess winter mortality **105**.5; **110**.19
    formal procedures **116**.29-32
    from heart disease **113**.19
    homeless people **79**.32
    in hospital **116**.31
    infant mortality **20**.28, 29, 30, 31; **105**.2

maternal mortality **20**.25, 28, 29, 30, 36, 37, 39
    missing persons **79**.14
    older people, winter **110**.19
    registering **116**.31
    in road accidents **119**.4, 5, 30
    from smoking **86**.2, 9, 10, 14, 16, 17
    unexpected **116**.31
    from water-related diseases **76**.2, 9, 13, 14, 20, 35
debit cards **43**.24, 29
    and the cashless society **74**.9-11
    and young people **74**.23-4
debt
    attitudes to **74**.5
    buying on credit **43**.29
    calculating total repayments **74**.26
    communication with creditors **74**.25
    and families **74**.3, 5-6
    getting out of **74**.16
    and lone parents **75**.37, 38
    managing **74**.34-5
    repayments **98**.3, 7-8, 31, 38, 39
    seeking help with **43**.33-4
    students **74**.3, 5, 19-20, 31-2, 34-9
        amounts of debt **74**.36
        calculating essential expenditure **74**.34
        coping with **74**.28-9, 34-5
        court and summonses **74**.35
        and credit cards **74**.3, 30, 32, 36, 37
        maximising your income **74**.34
        overdrafts **74**.1, 21-2
        priority debts **74**.34-5
    and unauthorised money lenders **74**.24
    women and debt problems **43**.30-1, 38-9
    world debt **110**.27-8
        public opinions **110**.34
    and young people **74**.1, 2, 15, 16, 23
decision-making
    children's participation in **120**.9-11
    and self-esteem **117**.37
deer hunting **103**.24, 28, 29
deforestation **78**.11, 18; **95**.4, 5, 13, 15
    and global warming **95**.4, 5, 13, 15
    and population growth **20**.1, 14, 23, 24
    and water shortages **76**.21, 36
degree performance, gender differences **112**.1, 8
dementia
    and advance directives **102**.33, 36
    Alzheimer's disease **84**.11-12
    and capacity **105**.39
    causes and prevention **105**.37
    and depression **105**.38; **125**.5
    missing persons suffering from **79**.13, 14
    and people in care homes **105**.15
    preventing **105**.30
    statistics **105**.3, 5, 37; **125**.16
    symptoms of **84**.12
    see also Alzheimer's disease
dental dams **96**.2; **101**.4
deportation as anti-terrorism measure **120**.38-9
depressant drugs **114**.1, 5, 29
depression **84**.6-7; **125**.1-23

and abortion **126**.11
and alcohol consumption **93**.28
and assisted suicide **102**.6, 7, 30, 31
attitudes to **84**.19-20, 21
and cannabis **80**.7, 16, 22
causes of **84**.6; **125**.2, 6, 19, 23
in children and young people **84**.29; **123**.27-8; **125**.8, 9, 27-8
clinical **84**.9
and complementary therapies **81**.30, 31; **125**.20, 39
drug treatment for **84**.19
endogenous **125**.4
and exam stress **100**.7
genetic factors in **125**.2
and grief **116**.5, 19
and homeless young people **79**.33, 36
and incapacity benefit **100**.23
manic depression *see* bipolar affective disorder
and men **125**.13-15
and obesity **113**.10
in older people **105**.38, 39; **125**.22-3
and personality **125**.2
and physical activity **113**.29-30; **125**.3, 20, 39
and physical illness **125**.2, 5-6
post-natal **84**.9; **125**.4, 17-18
reactive **125**.4
seeking help **125**.2-3
statistics on **84**.1
and stress **100**.1, 24
and suicide **77**.3; **125**.10
symptoms of **84**.3, 4, 6-7; **125**.1, 13
    in the elderly **125**.22-3
    manic depression **125**.19
    post-natal depression **125**.17
    seasonal affective disorder **125**.18
    teenagers **125**.8
treatment of **84**.35-6; **125**.24-39
    children and young people **125**.8, 27-8
    diet **125**.3, 39
    drugs **125**.7, 19, 22, 24-5, 32, 35
    ECT (electroconvulsive therapy) **125**.25-6, 34, 35
    elderly people **125**.23

manic depression **125**.19-20
post-natal depression **125**.17-18
psychotherapies **125**.29-31
Seasonal Affective Disorder **125**.18
self-help **125**.3, 39
talking therapies **125**.29-31
types of **84**.7; **125**.4
and underage drinking **125**.9
unipolar (endogenous) **125**.4, 10
and work performance **84**.23
see also bipolar affective disorder, (manic depression); seasonal affective disorder (SAD)
desertification, and water shortages **76**.21, 36
detention
    of children **120**.12; 17
    of refugee children **120**.21
detention centres **89**.12, 13
developing countries
    ageing population **20**.9, 11
    aid to **110**.28, 34
    AIDS/HIV in **96**.17-18, 36-7
    child labour in **99**.1, 2
    and climate change **95**.12-13, 14
    education in **20**.20, 28
     prohibitive cost **110**.38
        and urban growth **20**.18
        women and girls **20**.3, 9, 18
    and GM crops **87**.3, 4, 7, 28-30, 36
    life expectancy **20**.5
    population growth **20**.1-2, 4, 5, 8-9, 10
    and the right to water **76**.24-5, 32
    shantytowns **20**.17-18, 20
    and tourism **109**.32-3
        pro-poor **109**.27, 38
        responsible **109**.18-20, 30
        working conditions in the tourist industry **109**.30, 31, 32
    urban growth **20**.9, 11, 17-20, 33
    water collection **76**.13, 19-20
    water pollution **76**.4, 10
    water and sanitation services **76**.7, 8, 12, 17, 21
    water shortages **76**.16, 19, 21

Volume numbers appear first (in bold) followed by page numbers; a change in volume number is preceded by a semi-colon.

Vol. 19 Looking at Vegetarianism
Vol. 20 Population Growth
Vol. 22 Confronting Child Abuse
Vol. 29 Gambling
Vol. 43 A Consumer Society
Vol. 60 Confronting Cancer
Vol. 69 The Media
Vol. 74 Money Matters
Vol. 75 Lone-Parent Families
Vol. 76 The Water Crisis
Vol. 77 Self-inflicted Violence
Vol. 78 Threatened Species
Vol. 79 Dealing with Homelessness
Vol. 80 The Cannabis Debate
Vol. 81 Alternative Therapies
Vol. 82 Protecting our Privacy
Vol. 83 Dealing with Crime
Vol. 84 Mental Wellbeing
Vol. 85 The Housing Crisis
Vol. 86 Smoking and your Health
Vol. 87 Genetic Modification

Vol. 88 Food and Nutrition
Vol. 89 Refugees
Vol. 90 Human and Animal Cloning
Vol. 91 Disability Issues
Vol. 92 Terrorism
Vol. 93 Binge Drinking
Vol. 94 Religions and Beliefs in Britain
Vol. 95 The Climate Crisis
Vol. 96 Preventing Sexual Diseases
Vol. 97 Energy Matters
Vol. 98 The Globalisation Issue
Vol. 99 Exploited Children
Vol. 100 Stress and Anxiety
Vol. 101 Sexuality and Discrimination
Vol. 102 The Ethics of Euthanasia
Vol. 103 Animal Rights
Vol. 104 Our Internet Society
Vol. 105 Ageing Issues
Vol. 106 Trends in Marriage
Vol. 107 Work Issues
Vol. 108 Domestic Violence

Vol. 109 Responsible Tourism
Vol. 110 Poverty
Vol. 111 The Waste Problem
Vol. 112 Women, Men and Equality
Vol. 113 Fitness and Health
Vol. 114 Drug Abuse
Vol. 115 Racial Discrimination
Vol. 116 Grief and Loss
Vol. 117 Self-Esteem and Body Image
Vol. 118 Focus on Sport
Vol. 119 Transport Trends
Vol. 120 The Human Rights Issue
Vol. 121 The Censorship Debate
Vol. 122 Bullying
Vol. 123 Young People and Health
Vol. 124 Parenting Issues
Vol. 125 Understanding Depression
Vol. 126 The Abortion Debate
Vol. 127 Eating Disorders

and agriculture **76**.3, 4
and aid programmes **76**.5
statistics **76**.2, 6, 7
young people **20**.10-11, 33-4, 40
diabetes
and complementary therapies **81**.21
and exercise **113**.34
and obesity **113**.15; **127**.34
research **90**.18, 23-4
diarrhoea
and access to safe water and sanitation **76**.17
deaths from **76**.14, 30
and hygiene promotion **76**.6, 12
links to contaminated water **76**.5, 12
diet
and cancer **60**.1-5, 14
and cancer treatments **81**.32-3
and child behaviour **120**.16
and children **113**.4-5, 8
and coronary heart disease **113**.20
and depression **125**.3, 39
dietary trends **125**.11-12
fat in the diet **113**.14, 20
and life expectancy **105**.1-2, 9, 10
and mental ill-health **125**.11-12
and schizophrenia **84**.14-15
and Seasonal Affective Disorder **125**.38
and stress **100**.19, 30, 31, 35
teenage girls **117**.20, 21
and weight maintenance **113**.31-2
young people **123**.1, 6-7; 31
see also eating disorders; food and nutrition; healthy eating; vegetarian food
dietary obsession (orthorexia nervosa) **127**.19
dieting **113**.33
girls and young women **117**.20-21
direct debit **74**.9, 19, 24
direct racial discrimination **115**.7, 11
direct sex discrimination **112**.13
disability benefits **91**.3, 4, 11, 14
disabled persons tax credit **75**.38
disability and child poverty **110**.13
access audits **91**.14, 15-16
physical features adjustments **91**.13, 14
and service providers **91**.13-14
and smaller companies **91**.15-16
and workplace stress **100**.17, 20, 22
disabled babies
and abortion **126**.9, 34, 35
killing of newborn **102**.25
disabled children **91**.4, 18, 28, 29-30; **107**.21
disabled people
discrimination **91**.5, 6, 7, 12-25
and education **91**.7, 10, 29-36
and employment **91**.3, 4, 7, 10, 15-16, 19-20, 32; **107**.12
and football **118**.22
health provision **91**.11, 37-8, 39
housing **91**.11, 17
public attitudes to disability **91**.2-4
service and goods provision **91**.7, 8, 13-14

supplying cannabis to **80**.33
see also disability benefits; learning disabilities
discipline
parental **124**.2
in schools
and gender equality **112**.10
problems **120**.16
discrimination
and child labour **99**.4
direct and indirect **115**.7, 11
of disabled people **91**.5, 6, 7, 12-25
and mental illness **84**.19-20, 21-2
racial see racial discrimination
refugee children **120**.22
in the workplace **101**.23-4, 29, 35-6
see also ageism; prejudice; racism; religious discrimination; sex discrimination
disease
age-related diseases **105**.3, 32
and diet **19**.15, 19
and medical research **103**.12-13, 16
and population growth **20**.6, 19, 20
of poverty and wealth **110**.35
water-related **76**.2, 3, 5, 6, 9, 12, 19, 20, 35
and children **76**.2, 3, 5, 9, 13
displaced persons **89**.1, 6, 8-9
disposable nappies, environmental impact **111**.13-15
disruptive behaviour disorder, influence of media violence **121**.35
diuretics **118**.35, 37
diversity and sport **118**.12
divorce **106**.27-39
and children **124**.29-30, 31-32, 33-4
DIY abortions **126**.32-4
DIY burials **116**.38-9
DNA **87**.1-2, 18, 20, 22; **90**.2, 9
doctors
and abortion **126**.12, 13, 24
and cancer **60**.6, 7, 32, 38
cancer specialists (oncologists) **60**.14, 31, 36
and complementary medicine **60**.39; **81**.4
and euthanasia **102**.2, 4, 13, 14, 31
and help for eating disorders **127**.28
and help for problem drinkers **93**.28, 31
and medically assisted dying in the UK **102**.20-1
and reporting a death **116**.31
see also GPs (general practitioners); physician-assisted suicide (PAS)
domestic violence **83**.6; **108**.1-18; **112**.39; **124**.18
changing abusers' behaviour **108**.11-12, 33
cycle of abuse **108**.1, 11-12
definition **108**.1, 19, 24, 28
extent and facts about **108**.4, 7-8, 9-10, 19
helplines **108**.3, 14, 20, 21, 31, 37
injuries sustained **108**.9, 10
leaving home **108**.7-8, 9-10, 12, 21, 37
refuges **108**.32-33
legal protection **108**.38-9
living with abuse **108**.11, 15-16, 18
long-term effects **108**.1-2
and low self-esteem **108**.1, 2; **117**.32

male victims **108**.16, 17, 33
    reasons for abusive behaviour **108**.2, 22
    reporting to the police **108**.10, 36
    types of abuse **108**.5-7, 24
    women escaping from **79**.13, 37
domestic workers
    children as **99**.1, 4, 7-10
doorstep recycling **111**.3, 29
doping *see* drugs in sport
Down's syndrome **60**.10; **91**.2, 26, 27, 31
drink-driving **93**.22, 30, 31, 35, 36; **119**.8-9
    and drugs **114**.23-4
driver behaviour **119**.7-9
droughts, and climate change **95**.5, 9, 11, 14, 15, 19, 25, 26, 38
drug abuse **114**.1-30
    and HIV **96**.14, 26
    and homeless persons **79**.2, 10, 15
    and mental illness **84**.18
    parents' worries about **124**.17
    and self-harm **77**.10, 24, 26
    and suicide **77**.3, 4, 18, 23
    treatment **114**.10, 18-19
drug addiction **114**.17-19
drug development, and animal experiments **103**.2-3, 9, 10, 11, 13
drug testing **80**.2; **118**.25
    in schools **114**.26
    statistics **118**.33-4
    UK **118**.28, 30
drug treatments for depression **125**.7, 22, 32, 35
    manic depression **125**.19
drugs
    attitudes to illegal **43**.4
    classification **114**.1, 31, 33
    definition **114**.1
    depression caused by **125**.5-6, 10
    effects **114**.2, 29-30; **123**.8, 14
        crack **114**.10
        drug mixtures **114**.16-17
        ecstasy **114**.8, 29
        solvents **114**.27

and families of drug users **114**.25
    getting help **123**.14
    market and prices **114**.6-7
    trade **114**.6-7, 11-12, 33-5
    and young people **114**.20-28; **123**.1-2, 8, 9, 14
drugs and the law **114**.31-9
    legalisation debate **114**.39
    classifications of drugs **114**.1, 31, 33
    prosecution and punishment **114**.32, 35, 36
    see also cannabis
drugs in sport **118**.23-39
    anabolic steroids **118**.35, 36
    androstenedione **118**.35
    athletes' responsibilities **118**.32-3
    beta-blockers **118**.37
    caffeine **118**.35
    cannabinoids **118**.38
    clenbuterol **118**.35
    consequences of abuse **118**.32, 24
    diuretics **118**.35, 37
    effects of drugs **118**.35-8
    ephedrine **118**.35
    erythropoetin **118**.35
    history of **118**.23-5
    hormones **118**.37
    medication and banned substances **118**.32-3
    nadrolone precursors **118**.35
    nalbuphine **118**.35
    narcotic analgesics **118**.38
    peptide hormones and analogues **118**.37
    pressure to take drugs **118**.28-9
    stimulants **118**.36-7
    see also drug testing

E

email
    bullying **122**.5, 19, 21
    personal emails in the workplace **104**.15
    phishing **104**.32-3

Volume numbers appear first (in bold) followed by page numbers; a change in volume number is preceded by a semi-colon.

Vol. **19** Looking at Vegetarianism
Vol. **20** Population Growth
Vol. **22** Confronting Child Abuse
Vol. **29** Gambling
Vol. **43** A Consumer Society
Vol. **60** Confronting Cancer
Vol. **69** The Media
Vol. **74** Money Matters
Vol. **75** Lone-Parent Families
Vol. **76** The Water Crisis
Vol. **77** Self-inflicted Violence
Vol. **78** Threatened Species
Vol. **79** Dealing with Homelessness
Vol. **80** The Cannabis Debate
Vol. **81** Alternative Therapies
Vol. **82** Protecting our Privacy
Vol. **83** Dealing with Crime
Vol. **84** Mental Wellbeing
Vol. **85** The Housing Crisis
Vol. **86** Smoking and your Health
Vol. **87** Genetic Modification

Vol. **88** Food and Nutrition
Vol. **89** Refugees
Vol. **90** Human and Animal Cloning
Vol. **91** Disability Issues
Vol. **92** Terrorism
Vol. **93** Binge Drinking
Vol. **94** Religions and Beliefs in Britain
Vol. **95** The Climate Crisis
Vol. **96** Preventing Sexual Diseases
Vol. **97** Energy Matters
Vol. **98** The Globalisation Issue
Vol. **99** Exploited Children
Vol. **100** Stress and Anxiety
Vol. **101** Sexuality and Discrimination
Vol. **102** The Ethics of Euthanasia
Vol. **103** Animal Rights
Vol. **104** Our Internet Society
Vol. **105** Ageing Issues
Vol. **106** Trends in Marriage
Vol. **107** Work Issues
Vol. **108** Domestic Violence

Vol. **109** Responsible Tourism
Vol. **110** Poverty
Vol. **111** The Waste Problem
Vol. **112** Women, Men and Equality
Vol. **113** Fitness and Health
Vol. **114** Drug Abuse
Vol. **115** Racial Discrimination
Vol. **116** Grief and Loss
Vol. **117** Self-Esteem and Body Image
Vol. **118** Focus on Sport
Vol. **119** Transport Trends
Vol. **120** The Human Rights Issue
Vol. **121** The Censorship Debate
Vol. **122** Bullying
Vol. **123** Young People and Health
Vol. **124** Parenting Issues
Vol. **125** Understanding Depression
Vol. **126** The Abortion Debate
Vol. **127** Eating Disorders

spam **82**.31-3, 36-7; **104**.30-1

    surveillance of

        and the Government **82**.1, 22, 23

        in the workplace **82**.25, 26, 27, 28, 30; **120**.32

early medical abortion (EMA) 14, 33

earnings gap **110**.16; **112**.16-17

eating disorders **84**.9, 21; **117**.17-18; **123**.7, 33-4;
    127.1-31

    binge eating **117**.2, 15-16

    and body image **117**.27

    causes **117**.2-3, 6-7

    children **117**.3, 20-21

    and compulsive exercise **113**.38

    health risks **117**.4-5

    prevention programmes **117**.15, 18

    signs and symptoms **117**.2, 3, 17-19

        anorexia **117**.1, 2

        binge eating **117**.15, 16

        body dysmorphic disorder **117**.18-19

        bulimia **117**.1-2, 13, 14

    support for sufferers **117**.25-6, 28-30

    treatment **117**.28-9

        binge eating **117**.16

        bulimia **117**.14

        obesity **117**.34

    see also anorexia nervosa; bulimia nervosa; obesity

eco-systems

    degradation of freshwater **76**.35

    and water consumption **76**.2, 16-17, 19

economic equality, Britain's ranking **112**.29

economic growth **98**.16

    and global warming **95**.9, 11, 16-17

    and poverty reduction **110**.29

economic hardship following divorce, effect on children
    124.34

economic inequality, and terrorism **92**.13, 21

economic wealth and cultural poverty **110**.23

economy and refugees **89**.21, 22, 30-1

ecotourism **109**.19-20, 38-9

ecstasy (MDMA) **114**.4-5, 8

    deaths from **80**.10, 11

    and depression **125**.10

    effects of **114**.8, 29

    mixed with other drugs **114**.16, 17

    possession of **114**.33

    prices **114**.6

    users, influence of parenting style **114**.24

    young users **114**.22

ECT (electro-convulsive therapy) **84**.36; **125**.25-6, 34, 35

ectomorph body shape **127**.22

education

    and behaviour problems in schools **120**.16

    and black history **115**.16-17

    and black pupils **115**.19-21

    and child labour **99**.3, 7, 15; **120**.18-19

    and child soldiers **99**.31

    and children's rights **120**.11

    costs **124**.3

    in developing countries **20**.20, 28;

        costs **110**.38

    and disabled people **91**.7, 10, 29-36

    faith-based schools **94**.12-14, 28, 30-1

    and gender **112**.1-11

    global gender inequality **112**.39

    inequalities **110**.14

    in mental health **84**.4, 30-2

    and minority ethnic pupils **115**.18

    in money matters **74**.1, 5-6, 12, 13

    and online learning **104**.9-10, 11

    and racial integration **115**.29, 30, 37

    and racism **115**.19-20

    RE (religious education) **94**.9-10, 15, 31

    sex discrimination **112**.13-14

    and teenage parents **75**.1, 2

    and young people with HIV/AIDS **96**.26, 32, 33

    young people's attitudes to **123**.2

    see also schools; sex education; students; teachers;
    universities

educational achievement

    gender differences **112**.1, 8, 11

efficiency from reducing waste **111**.18

elderly people

    and cancer **60**.3, 7, 14

    and dementia **84**.11, 12

    and depression **125**.22-3

    growth in numbers of **20**.9, 11

    and homelessness **79**.9

    and housing **85**.2, 10, 15

    lesbian, gay and bisexual **101**.9-10

    and mental health problems **84**.1

    and poverty **110**.19-20

    see also grandparents; older people

electric vehicles **119**.21-2

electricity generation from waste **111**.39

electro-convulsive therapy (ECT) **84**.36; **125**.25-6, 34, 35

electronic equipment recycling **111**.31, 35

elephants

    ivory trade **78**.20

    killing of **78**.4, 6, 19

eliminating poverty **110**.23

embryo cloning *see* human reproductive cloning

embryo rights **90**.5

embryo-splitting **90**.2-3

emergency contraception (EC) **75**.3, 13, 15-16, 17;
    126.24

emissions, transport **119**.1, 15, 31

    aircraft **119**.16

    and climate change **119**.14, 24, 30

emotional abuse **108**.1, 6-7, 13, 19

emotional blackmail by parents **124**.15

emotional changes, and stress **100**.33

emotional disorders, young people **125**.9

    symptoms **84**.30-1

emotional problems, sharing **123**.10

emotions and gender differences **112**.32-3

emphysema **86**.6, 9

employees

    and Internet addiction **104**.37

    and personal email **104**.15

employers

    and ageism in the workforce **105**.23-4, 26, 27

    equality policies **115**.13

and privacy rights in the workplace 82.25-30
and sexual orientation monitoring 101.24
and workplace stress 100.17-18, 20
employment
    and ageism 105.4, 16-27
    of disabled people 91.3, 4, 7, 10, 15-16, 19-20, 32
    and gender 112.12-27
    and lone parents 75.30, 38
    and obesity 113.17
    of parents as factor in child poverty 110.12
    and students 74.20, 29, 37
    in urban areas in the developing world 20.18, 19-20
    working conditions 98.4, 13, 14, 17, 25-6
employment and racism 115.12, 13
employment of refugees 89.22-3, 24, 26-7, 32
    illegal employment of refugees 89.10-11, 30-1
empty houses
    and environmental decline 85.14
    numbers of 85.25, 29
    and the vacancy rate 85.9, 25
endangered species 78.1-3
    birds 78.2, 8-9, 27, 29, 37
    and climate change 95.22
    and cloning 90.21, 30
    and the killing of wildlife 78.2, 4-5, 5-6
    mammals 78.3, 27, 28, 32
    plants 78.2-3, 7, 17, 21, 36
    and pollution 78.6
    trade in 78.16-17, 19-22, 38-9
    in the UK 78.28-31
    see also conservation; extinction; wildlife
endocrine disorders and depression 125.5
endogenous (unipolar) depression 84.7; 125.4, 10
energy
    and the countryside 97.24-5
    output of the energy industry 97.3
    production and supply 97.3-4
    public attitudes to energy and environment 97.34-6
    saving through recycling 111.28, 30, 32
    from waste 111.2, 3, 39
energy consumption 87.24, 25; 97.6
energy efficiency 95.5, 28, 29-32; 97.27-33

future of 95.28
and global warming 97.29
green electricity 95.32
in the home 95.29, 30-1, 32; 97.2, 27-30, 31, 32-3
in industry 95.34
and renewable energy sources 97.11
and shopping 97.31-2
and sustainable housing 85.37
and transport 95.5, 27, 28, 34; 97.24, 25, 31
in the workplace 95.32
see also renewable energy
entrepreneurs 107.4
environment
    carbon dioxide emissions 98.14
    destruction, contributing to hunger 110.30-31
    and economic growth 98.16
    and housing 85.14-15, 26
        see also sustainable housing
    and population growth 20.1, 4, 8, 22-4
        resource depletion 20.2, 3, 6
        water shortages 20.6, 9, 13-14, 22, 23, 24
    protection of 88.32, 34, 35
    public attitudes to 97.34
    use of resources to combat poverty 110.25-6
    and self-esteem 117.37, 38-9
    and vegetarianism 19.6-7, 26, 27, 33
    and water bills 76.33, 34
    see also sustainable development; wildlife
environmentally cleaner vehicles 119.20-23
ephedrine 118.35
epidemiology (population studies) 103.17, 18, 19, 22
epilepsy 91.28
equal opportunity in sport 118.12-13, 15-16, 18-19, 22
equal pay 112.13, 20
    gender pay gap 107.13, 25, 26; 112.16-17
equity in sport 118.12
    gender equity 118.18-19
erythropoetin (EPO) 118.35, 37
escalation theory of drug use 114.39
escharotics (cancer salves) 81.33
ethical trade 98.3, 6
ethnic minorities

Volume numbers appear first (in bold) followed by page numbers; a change in volume number is preceded by a semi-colon.

Vol. 19 Looking at Vegetarianism
Vol. 20 Population Growth
Vol. 22 Confronting Child Abuse
Vol. 29 Gambling
Vol. 43 A Consumer Society
Vol. 60 Confronting Cancer
Vol. 69 The Media
Vol. 74 Money Matters
Vol. 75 Lone-Parent Families
Vol. 76 The Water Crisis
Vol. 77 Self-inflicted Violence
Vol. 78 Threatened Species
Vol. 79 Dealing with Homelessness
Vol. 80 The Cannabis Debate
Vol. 81 Alternative Therapies
Vol. 82 Protecting our Privacy
Vol. 83 Dealing with Crime
Vol. 84 Mental Wellbeing
Vol. 85 The Housing Crisis
Vol. 86 Smoking and your Health
Vol. 87 Genetic Modification

Vol. 88 Food and Nutrition
Vol. 89 Refugees
Vol. 90 Human and Animal Cloning
Vol. 91 Disability Issues
Vol. 92 Terrorism
Vol. 93 Binge Drinking
Vol. 94 Religions and Beliefs in Britain
Vol. 95 The Climate Crisis
Vol. 96 Preventing Sexual Diseases
Vol. 97 Energy Matters
Vol. 98 The Globalisation Issue
Vol. 99 Exploited Children
Vol. 100 Stress and Anxiety
Vol. 101 Sexuality and Discrimination
Vol. 102 The Ethics of Euthanasia
Vol. 103 Animal Rights
Vol. 104 Our Internet Society
Vol. 105 Ageing Issues
Vol. 106 Trends in Marriage
Vol. 107 Work Issues
Vol. 108 Domestic Violence

Vol. 109 Responsible Tourism
Vol. 110 Poverty
Vol. 111 The Waste Problem
Vol. 112 Women, Men and Equality
Vol. 113 Fitness and Health
Vol. 114 Drug Abuse
Vol. 115 Racial Discrimination
Vol. 116 Grief and Loss
Vol. 117 Self-Esteem and Body Image
Vol. 118 Focus on Sport
Vol. 119 Transport Trends
Vol. 120 The Human Rights Issue
Vol. 121 The Censorship Debate
Vol. 122 Bullying
Vol. 123 Young People and Health
Vol. 124 Parenting Issues
Vol. 125 Understanding Depression
Vol. 126 The Abortion Debate
Vol. 127 Eating Disorders

and attitudes to advertising **69**.14

British identity **115**.38

and education **115**.18

and football **118**.13-16

and homelessness **79**.10, 19

and identity cards **82**.2, 8

mixed race population in the UK **115**.24-5

and poverty **110**.2

religious identity **94**.3, 5

and teenage parenthood **75**.2, 23

as victims of crime **115**.10

see also Asian people; black people; employment and racism; racism

ethnic origin

and body image **117**.29-30

and child poverty **110**.12

as grounds for discrimination **115**.7

young people and sex **123**.19-20

euthanasia

active or direct **102**.1, 2

and advance directives (living wills) **102**.18, 29, 32, 33-9

arguments against **102**.13-14, 28-9, 30-1

arguments for **102**.12-13, 15

and compassion **102**.12-13, 30

defining **102**.1

indirect **102**.1

involuntary **102**.1

law on **102**.5, 7, 8, 10, 15-16, 19

and medical technology **102**.1, 3, 29, 30, 31

non-religious perspective on **102**.1-2

non-voluntary **102**.1

and quality of life **102**.2, 29, 30

religious views on **102**.2, 8-9, 12-14, 17, 18

see also advance directives; assisted suicide; physician-assisted suicide (PAS)

exam stress **100**.3-7; **123**.29-30

causes of **100**.5

dealing with **100**.5, 6

getting help and advice with **100**.3

exercise **88**.1, 2-3, 11, 12, 18; **113**.10, 21-30, 34-9

aerobic exercise **113**.22

barriers to **113**.25

benefits of **113**.21, 22-3, 25, 30; **118**.3

for women **118**.20

children **113**.1, 6, 8; **119**.31

compulsive **113**.37-8

and depression **113**.29-30; **125**.3, 20, 39

and emotional health and wellbeing **84**.24, 27; **113**.22

and the heart **113**.34

and life expectancy **105**.31

motivation for **113**.26, 35

recommended amounts **113**.22-3, 25-6, 27, 31, 37

children **113**.1

and self-esteem **117**.37, 38

and stress

benefits of **100**.19, 27, 30, 34, 36, 37

and weight reduction **113**.31

and young people **123**.2, 7

exploitation of workers **120**.28-31

external costs of motoring **119**.14

extreme poverty **110**.21

F

facial recognition technology **82**.3, 6, 17

and identity cards **82**.9, 10

factory farming **19**.24, 30-1, 35-6, 37-8

fair trade **98**.3, 38; **109**.31; **110**.32-3

faith differences and relationships **115**.39

faith hate crime **115**.27

families

and body image **117**.14

changing family patterns **106**.1-2; **124**.20-39

and debt problems **74**.3, 5-6

of drug users **114**.25

family breakdowns

and domestic violence **79**.37

and homeless young people **79**.36

and missing persons **79**.13-14

and young runaways **79**.24, 25

homeless **79**.4, 11, 19, 33

of lesbians and gays

coming out to **101**.2-3, 11, 12, 13

problems **124**.18

young people's worries **123**.3

reaction to mixed-faith relationships **115**.39

and relationship support **106**.29-30

size

and child poverty **110**.13

influenced by costs of raising children **124**.18

and suicide **77**.33, 36-8

and teenage parenthood **75**.2

and working women **112**.20

and working parents **124**.1, 21

see also lone parents; parents; stepfamilies

family planning **20**.11, 25-40

and the education of girls **20**.3, 9

international conferences and programmes **20**.21, 25-6, 28, 36-8, 39-40

and maternal mortality **20**.25, 28, 29, 30

and population growth **20**.3, 10

and reproductive rights **20**.27-8, 35

and sexual health **20**.27, 28, 33-5, 39-40

see also birth control; contraception

fashion, and the fur trade **103**.36-7

fast foods

and litter **111**.12

and teenagers **43**.6, 7

fat intake **88**.2, 5, 7, 8

in the diet **113**.14, 20

and food labelling **88**.21-2, 22-3

teenagers **123**.7

fathers

and abortion **126**.13, 15-16

absent

relationships with children **75**.36

and childcare **124**.7-11

impact on children's achievement **124**.7

employment patterns **107**.24-5

full-time fathers **124**.9-10
and household tasks **124**.11
lone fathers **75**.28, 34-6
new fathers and depression **125**.14
paternity leave **107**.25
separated
and debt **75**.37
relationships with children **75**.36
unmarried, and parental responsibility **124**.4
working fathers **107**.24-25
young fathers
and paid paternity leave **75**.12
and parental responsibility **75**.12
socio-economic background **75**.1, 2
fear of crime **83**.6, 38
and young people **83**.16, 17
fear of terrorism **92**.3-5, 13
fear after traumatic bereavement **116**.11-12
feelings
after bereavement **116**.1, 3-4, 5, 7-9, 10-11, 19, 21-2, 30
healthy self-esteem **117**.30
low self-esteem **117**.5
foetus
abnormality and abortion **126**.9, 35
development of **126**.26
feeling pain **126**.22, 26
rights **126**.21-2, 27
viability **126**.27
fibre intake **88**.2, 5, 6, 23
films
classification **121**.22, 23-5, 29-30
violence, and playground bullying **121**.28
financial abuse **108**.7, 15
and older people **105**.13
first-time buyers, and house prices **85**.6, 7
fish oils, and schizophrenia **84**.14-15
fisheries, and climate change **95**.3, 7, 28
fitness **113**.21, 24, 26, 27-8
benefits of walking **113**.39
motivation **113**.35
young people **123**.2
see also exercise

flashbacks (drug use) **114**.29-30
flexible working **98**.17; **107**.2, 11-12, 14-19
in an ageing society **105**.19-20, 27
and gender equality **112**.20
right to request **107**.17-18, 21-2
flooding
and climate change **95**.1, 3, 5, 7, 9, 11, 12, 19, 38
flash floods **95**.25, 38
impact of **95**.14, 25
in the UK **95**.26
fly-tipping **111**.3, 9, 19, 20, 21
food
and animal cloning **90**.39
and energy efficiency **97**.32, 33
expenditure on **43**.1, 3, 13
and population growth **20**.2-3, 6, 8, 13, 24
production and climate change **95**.1, 9, 11, 14, 15, 16
production and global water supplies **76**.3, 4, 7, 18
and religion **94**.10
in schools, attitudes to **123**.32
supplies in developing countries **20**.18, 24; **110**.30
and young people **123**.1
see also diet; eating disorders; fast foods; fat intake;
healthy eating; meat consumption; vegetarian food
food companies **98**.28-9, 30
food labelling **87**.3-4, 5, 6, 9, 11, 13, 32; **88**.9, 21-5
food and nutrition **88**.1-39
additives **88**.13-14, 34, 36, 38, 39
advertising and promotion **88**.10, 11, 19, 20, 35, 37
food poisoning **88**.14, 27-9
food safety **88**.26, 32, 34
healthy diet **88**.1-2, 5-7
junk food **88**.9-11
locally grown produce **88**.31, 33
nutrition information panels **88**.21, 22-3
teenagers **123**.6-7
and vegan diets **19**.12, 13-14
and vegetarian diets **19**.3, 9
food poisoning **88**.14, 27-9; **95**.28
and animal products **19**.3, 7, 16
food weaknesses, Britain **113**.13-14
foot-and-mouth disease

Volume numbers appear first (in bold) followed by page numbers; a change in volume number is preceded by a semi-colon.

Vol. **19** Looking at Vegetarianism
Vol. **20** Population Growth
Vol. **22** Confronting Child Abuse
Vol. **29** Gambling
Vol. **43** A Consumer Society
Vol. **60** Confronting Cancer
Vol. **69** The Media
Vol. **74** Money Matters
Vol. **75** Lone-Parent Families
Vol. **76** The Water Crisis
Vol. **77** Self-inflicted Violence
Vol. **78** Threatened Species
Vol. **79** Dealing with Homelessness
Vol. **80** The Cannabis Debate
Vol. **81** Alternative Therapies
Vol. **82** Protecting our Privacy
Vol. **83** Dealing with Crime
Vol. **84** Mental Wellbeing
Vol. **85** The Housing Crisis
Vol. **86** Smoking and your Health
Vol. **87** Genetic Modification

Vol. **88** Food and Nutrition
Vol. **89** Refugees
Vol. **90** Human and Animal Cloning
Vol. **91** Disability Issues
Vol. **92** Terrorism
Vol. **93** Binge Drinking
Vol. **94** Religions and Beliefs in Britain
Vol. **95** The Climate Crisis
Vol. **96** Preventing Sexual Diseases
Vol. **97** Energy Matters
Vol. **98** The Globalisation Issue
Vol. **99** Exploited Children
Vol. **100** Stress and Anxiety
Vol. **101** Sexuality and Discrimination
Vol. **102** The Ethics of Euthanasia
Vol. **103** Animal Rights
Vol. **104** Our Internet Society
Vol. **105** Ageing Issues
Vol. **106** Trends in Marriage
Vol. **107** Work Issues
Vol. **108** Domestic Violence

Vol. **109** Responsible Tourism
Vol. **110** Poverty
Vol. **111** The Waste Problem
Vol. **112** Women, Men and Equality
Vol. **113** Fitness and Health
Vol. **114** Drug Abuse
Vol. **115** Racial Discrimination
Vol. **116** Grief and Loss
Vol. **117** Self-Esteem and Body Image
Vol. **118** Focus on Sport
Vol. **119** Transport Trends
Vol. **120** The Human Rights Issue
Vol. **121** The Censorship Debate
Vol. **122** Bullying
Vol. **123** Young People and Health
Vol. **124** Parenting Issues
Vol. **125** Understanding Depression
Vol. **126** The Abortion Debate
Vol. **127** Eating Disorders

and the ban on hunting **103**.26
and rural tourism in England **109**.25
and vegetarianism **19**.22
football
and disabled people **118**.22
and homophobia **118**.17
racial equality **118**.13-16
and violence **118**.7, 8
wages **118**.11
football pools
age restrictions **29**.18, 27
expenditure on **29**.9
and men **29**.8, 9
online **29**.12
forced labour **120**.28-30
children **120**.18-19
forced marriages **106**.15; **108**.24
foreign investment **98**.17-18, 25
forestry
afforestation **95**.5
and climate change **95**.2, 3, 4, 7, 15, 39
forest fires **95**.4, 10
regeneration of tropical rainforests **95**.2
threatened species of animals in **78**.1, 2, 5
see also deforestation
fossil fuels **87**.24
alternatives to reliance on **97**.2, 21
as an energy source **97**.8, 21
and biomass **97**.18
burning **95**.2, 4, 6, 9, 10, 25, 38
and energy efficiency **95**.20, 34
see also oil
fraud **43**.26-7
credit card **43**.26-7
and identity cards **82**.2, 7, 8, 11, 12
preventing **43**.34-7
fraud on the Internet **43**.26, 28, 39-40
free press **121**.1-2
free speech **121**.1-21
and the Internet **121**.18, 19
and law **121**.7
timeline **121**.3
free trade **98**.3, 10-11, 16-17, 22, 31
see also trade liberalisation
freedom of expression **121**.4
and cartoons of Mohammed **121**.10-13, 15-16
French Revolution, and terror **92**.1, 6-7, 10, 14
friends
bullied, how to help **122**.13
with eating disorders, how to help **127**.30
as family **124**.19
support for manic depressives **125**.20
fruit machines
age and the law **29**.27
expenditure on **29**.9
and men **29**.8
and problem gamblers **29**.35, 36, 40
fuel cell vehicles **119**.22-3
fuel efficient cars **119**.20-23
fuel taxes **119**.14, 24
aircraft **119**.16

fuels, cleaner **119**.20-23
full-time fathers **124**.9-10
full-time mothers, working hours **124**.12
funerals **116**.3, 16, 20, 33-5
alternative **116**.38-9
arranging **116**.32
children's questions about **116**.26
and young people **116**.23
furniture recycling **111**.35-6

G

G8 protests **121**.14
gambling **29**.1-40
age restrictions on **29**.27
bingo **29**.2, 3, 7, 8, 9, 18, 22, 27
bookmaker bets **29**.7, 9, 12
dog racing **29**.2, 8, 9
expenditure on **29**.8-9, 17
football pools **29**.3, 7, 8, 9, 12, 18, 27
fruit machines **29**.1, 2, 7, 8, 9, 35, 36, 40
horse racing **29**.2, 3, 7, 8, 9, 19
international comparisons **29**.1-2, 7, 9
online gambling **29**.3, 4, 7, 10-16, 23, 25
participation in
and age **29**.8
in Britain **29**.7-9
and gender **29**.3, 8
and social class **29**.3, 8, 13
private bets **29**.7, 8
problem gamblers **29**.35; **123**.8
UK law on
liberalisation **29**.1, 16, 17, 18-19, 22-3
online gambling **29**.12
and women **29**.3, 8, 9, 26
and young people **29**.2, 37-8
see also casinos; compulsive gambling; National Lottery
gang culture **83**.11-12
gap years **107**.27
garden waste recycling **111**.16, 31, 33
gardens and water conservation **76**.1, 36, 37, 38
gay couples
reproduction and human cloning **90**.21
gay men
acceptance of **112**.38
and anal sex **101**.3-4
coming out **101**.11-13
and depression **125**.15
and the history of the LGBT community **101**.28-9
and HIV **96**.17, 20, 23
and the law **101**.5
age of consent **101**.3, 9, 27
and sexually transmitted infections (STIs) **96**.3, 4, 10, 12
see also homosexuality
GCSE performance, gender differences **112**.1, 8
GDP (Gross Domestic Product) **98**.14, 16
gender

and ageism in employment **105**.22

and bullying **122**.18

and car use **119**.29

and debt problems **43**.30

and depression **125**.2

development **112**.28, 35

and employment **112**.12-27

and life expectancy **105**.2, 9-10

and participation in gambling **29**.3, 8, 9

and society **112**.28-39

and stress **100**.13, 19

see also equal pay; men; women

gender-based violence **112**.39

see also domestic violence; rape

gender and education **112**.1-11

and educational performance **112**.1, 8, 11

and examination results **112**.1, 8

higher education **112**.1, 8

vocational training **112**.1, 21-2

gender equality

and boys **112**.33-4

and careers options **112**.9, 20, 21-2, 23-7

in education **112**.9-11

gender equity in sport **118**.18-19

gender gap

educational achievement **112**.1, 7, 8, 11

employment **112**.18, 20

international comparisons **112**.29

gender identity **101**.7

gender pay gap **112**.16-17

gender stereotyping **108**.26; **112**.35

in education **112**.11

at work **112**.15

gender and work **112**.12-27

careers options **112**.9, 20, 21-2, 23-7

and equal pay **112**.13, 20

pay gap **112**.16-17

gene doping **118**.34

gene therapy **118**.39

genes **87**.1-2

and depression 2

and eating disorders **127**.6-7

fertility genes and homosexuality **101**.8

gene pharming **90**.29-30, 32, 35

inserting **87**.2, 17, 22

and obesity **113**.9; **127**.35

switching off **87**.2, 20; **90**.2

therapy **90**.11

transfer from GM food to body cells **87**.8, 17, 33

genetic engineering **90**.21

and the postponement of ageing **105**.31-3

genetically modified animals, experiments on **103**.1, 8

genetically modified (GM) crops **19**.7; **88**.14, 32, 33

allergenicity of GM crops **87**.8, 17, 18, 19-20

benefits of GM crops **87**.7, 8, 22, 24, 25

Britain and GM crops **87**.14-16

commercial crop growing **87**.10, 31

consumer attitudes to **87**.3-4, 5-7, 16

cross-contamination **87**.18, 20, 21, 30, 31-2

developing countries **87**.3, 4, 7, 28-30, 36

economic benefits **87**.4, 7

environmental risks/benefits **87**.7, 8, 14-16, 19-20, 25

health risks/benefits **87**.7, 8, 17-20, 33

legislation **87**.6, 10-11, 30

non-food crops **87**.20, 37-8

profitability from GM crops **87**.15, 31

public opinion **87**.3-4, 5-7, 16

regulations **87**.6, 10-11, 30

safety controls **87**.6, 8, 9, 17, 30, 39

testing procedures **87**.10, 17, 18

genetics research **103**.11, 13

genital herpes **96**.3, 4

and HIV **96**.12

genital warts **96**.2-3, 4, 12-13

Genito-Urinary Medicine (GUM) clinics **96**.1, 10

health advisers and safer sex **96**.1, 10

and HIV testing **96**.16

pressure on services **96**.3, 4, 8-9, 11

tests and treatment offered at **96**.10

and sexually transmitted infections **123**.25

geothermal energy **97**.6-7, 9, 11-12

germs **88**.27, 28-9

GHB (gammahydroxybutyrate) **114**.31

and drug mixing **114**.17

Volume numbers appear first (in bold) followed by page numbers; a change in volume number is preceded by a semi-colon.

Vol. 19 Looking at Vegetarianism

Vol. 20 Population Growth

Vol. 22 Confronting Child Abuse

Vol. 29 Gambling

Vol. 43 A Consumer Society

Vol. 60 Confronting Cancer

Vol. 69 The Media

Vol. 74 Money Matters

Vol. 75 Lone-Parent Families

Vol. 76 The Water Crisis

Vol. 77 Self-inflicted Violence

Vol. 78 Threatened Species

Vol. 79 Dealing with Homelessness

Vol. 80 The Cannabis Debate

Vol. 81 Alternative Therapies

Vol. 82 Protecting our Privacy

Vol. 83 Dealing with Crime

Vol. 84 Mental Wellbeing

Vol. 85 The Housing Crisis

Vol. 86 Smoking and your Health

Vol. 87 Genetic Modification

Vol. 88 Food and Nutrition

Vol. 89 Refugees

Vol. 90 Human and Animal Cloning

Vol. 91 Disability Issues

Vol. 92 Terrorism

Vol. 93 Binge Drinking

Vol. 94 Religions and Beliefs in Britain

Vol. 95 The Climate Crisis

Vol. 96 Preventing Sexual Diseases

Vol. 97 Energy Matters

Vol. 98 The Globalisation Issue

Vol. 99 Exploited Children

Vol. 100 Stress and Anxiety

Vol. 101 Sexuality and Discrimination

Vol. 102 The Ethics of Euthanasia

Vol. 103 Animal Rights

Vol. 104 Our Internet Society

Vol. 105 Ageing Issues

Vol. 106 Trends in Marriage

Vol. 107 Work Issues

Vol. 108 Domestic Violence

Vol. 109 Responsible Tourism

Vol. 110 Poverty

Vol. 111 The Waste Problem

Vol. 112 Women, Men and Equality

Vol. 113 Fitness and Health

Vol. 114 Drug Abuse

Vol. 115 Racial Discrimination

Vol. 116 Grief and Loss

Vol. 117 Self-Esteem and Body Image

Vol. 118 Focus on Sport

Vol. 119 Transport Trends

Vol. 120 The Human Rights Issue

Vol. 121 The Censorship Debate

Vol. 122 Bullying

Vol. 123 Young People and Health

Vol. 124 Parenting Issues

Vol. 125 Understanding Depression

Vol. 126 The Abortion Debate

Vol. 127 Eating Disorders

ghettos **115**.28, 31

girls' schools **112**.4-5

girls and young women
  academic achievement **112**.1, 8, 11
  and alcohol **93**.16
    binge drinking **93**.1, 15, 19-20
  and body image **117**.14-15, 19, 20-21, 22, 25
  and bullying **122**.10, 14, 15-16
  and child abuse **22**.12, 13
  and child labour **99**.2, 3
  child soldiers **99**.29, 31, 36
  and cosmetic surgery **117**.26-8
  in developing countries **20**.25, 34
    education of **20**.3, 9; **110**.38
    and family planning **20**.29-30
  and dieting **117**.20-21
  and education
    examination results **112**.1, 8, 11
    single-sex teaching **112**.4-6
    vocational **112**.21-2
  and exercise
    overexercise **113**.23, 28
  and Internet access **104**.3
  and plastic surgery **117**.26-8
  prison custody and under 18s **83**.23, 27-9
  and puberty **127**.22
  self-esteem programmes **117**.13, 15
  and self-harm **77**.6-7, 20, 24
  sexual behaviour **20**.26, 34; **75**.17, 18, 19, 20
  sexual exploitation of **99**.16, 20, 21-2
  and sport **118**.20
  street children **99**.18-19
  and suicide **77**.2, 5

glaciers
  melting **95**.3, 7, 11, 14, 25, 26

glass ceiling **107**.9; **112**.15-16, 20

glass cliff **107**.9; **112**.20

glass recycling **111**.11, 23, 27, 28, 31, 36

Global Gag Rule **126**.19

global poverty **110**.21-39
  public opinions on **110**.34

global tourism
  and the air industry **109**.2
  destinations **109**.1
  growth of **109**.1-3, 7
  jobs created by **109**.1

global warming
  and air travel **109**.19
  causes of **95**.4, 9
  and changes in global climate zones **95**.14-15
  effects of **95**.5, 6-7, 9, 11-15
  and energy efficiency **97**.29
  global temperatures **95**.5, 6, 7, 8, 9, 10, 11, 12, 35, 38
  human influences on **95**.6, 25, 30, 33
  increase in **95**.2, 9, 10
  and population growth **20**.23, 24
  potential impact of **95**.2-3
  and renewable energy **97**.8
  see also climate change; energy efficiency; greenhouse gas emissions

globalisation **43**.10-11

benefits **98**.1, 12
and child labour **99**.14
and consumerism **43**.10-11
corporate globalisation **98**.25-7
definition **98**.12
effects of **98**.13-14
and poverty **98**.1, 13, 35-6
and the rich-poor gap **98**.33-4
and unemployment **98**.19-20, 32, 37

GM crops *see* genetically modified (GM) crops

gonorrhoea **96**.2, 3, 4, 8, 9, 10
  and HIV **96**.12

Google and Chinese censorship **121**.20-21

Government
  abortion time-limit review **126**.36-7
  control of the media **121**.1
  media censorship **121**.37
  use of the media **121**.17-18

Government policies
  on age discrimination **105**.18, 20, 23-4, 26
  on beggars **79**.26
  on cannabis
    advertising **80**.29-30
    for medicinal purposes **80**.26, 34
    reclassification of **80**.7, 8, 14, 18, 20, 24-6
  on child poverty **110**.2, 4, 6-7
  on child protection and the Internet **22**.39, 40
  crime reduction targets **83**.38
  on families
    children and divorce **106**.35-6
    and cohabitees **106**.7-8
    and marriage **106**.31
    and relationship support **106**.29-30
  on gambling
    betting taxes **29**.2, 17, 23, 36
    liberalisation of the law on **29**.1, 16, 17, 18-19, 22-3
    online gambling **29**.12
  on healthy eating **19**.4-5
  on homelessness **79**.3, 7
    young people **79**.24, 28-9
  housing
    and the environment **85**.15
    in rural areas **85**.5, 27-8, 31
  on ID cards **82**.7-12
  and the Internet
    child protection **104**.28-9
    closing the digital divide **104**.13
  on mental health **84**.36-7, 39
    in older people **105**.39
  on the physical punishment of children **22**.22, 23, 24, 25, 26-7
  on sex education **75**.18
  on social exclusion **110**.8-9
  on suicide **77**.18
    national suicide prevention strategy **77**.16, 19
  on surveillance **82**.1-3, 22, 23
  on teenage pregnancies **75**.1, 9, 13, 27
  on teenage sex **75**.17
  and yob-culture Britain **83**.5-6
  on young people's health **123**.31

Government targets

child poverty **110**.2, 4, 6-7
road safety **119**.4
GPs (general practitioners)
and the adverse affects of cannabis, advice to patients
80.18-19
and Alzheimer's disease **84**.11
and assisted suicide **102**.9, 15
and bereavement support **116**.2
and cancer **60**.31
breast cancer **60**.22, 23
childhood cancers **60**.10, 11
diagnosis **60**.14
in elderly people **60**.7
and complementary medicine **81**.21, 29, 34
and eating disorders **127**.28
help for problem drinkers **93**.28, 31
and mental illness **84**.10, 28
prescribing cannabis to patients
and the law **80**.7
support for **80**.5
seeking help for stress from **100**.2, 33, 34
graduates **107**.14-15, 35-6
construction industry **112**.25
gender gap **112**.1, 8
recruiting disabled graduates **91**.19-20
starting salaries **74**.31
graffiti, clearing up **83**.35
grandparents
and childcare **124**.1, 37-8
opinions of parenting skills **124**.2
Green Belt land **85**.28, 30, 31, 39
green burials **116**.39
green cars *see* fuel efficient cars
greenfield sites
house-building on **85**.9, 25
guidelines on **85**.28
and housing density **85**.34
and urban renewal **85**.35
greenhouse gas **111**.3
see also carbon dioxide emissions
grief **116**.1-2, 3-5, 7-9
counselling **116**.6

importance of grieving **116**.3
length of grieving process **116**.4-5
public **116**.17-18
and traumatic bereavement **116**.10-11
and young people **116**.19-28
growth and nutrition, teenagers **123**.6-7
guilt, feelings after bereavement **116**.4, 11, 19
children **116**.27
and traumatic bereavement **116**.11
gyms **113**.36

H

habitat loss
and endangered wildlife in Britain **78**.30-1, 32
hallucinogens **114**.2, 5, 29
happy slapping **122**.5, 26
harassment **122**.30
racial **115**.8
sexual **112**.11
hard segregation **115**.28
hare coursing **103**.25, 26, 27
hazardous waste **111**.3
hazardous work
and child labour **99**.1, 2, 3
domestic labour **99**.7
headteachers, and homophobia **101**.38-9
health
and alcohol **93**.4, 7, 8-9, 9, 18, 26, 28, 30
and beggars **79**.34, 35
and cannabis **80**.7, 10, 12, 13, 15; **114**.37
and the immune system **80**.19
lung damage **80**.18-19
and pregnant women **80**.15, 19
reclassification of **80**.29, 30
and climate change **95**.1, 3, 7, 11, 15, 23, 27
of cloned animals **90**.27, 28, 31, 34, 39
of cloned humans **90**.1, 2, 3, 7, 9
and cycling **119**.39
and eating disorders **127**.4-5

Volume numbers appear first (in bold) followed by page numbers; a change in volume number is preceded by a semi-colon.

Vol. **19** Looking at Vegetarianism
Vol. **20** Population Growth
Vol. **22** Confronting Child Abuse
Vol. **29** Gambling
Vol. **43** A Consumer Society
Vol. **60** Confronting Cancer
Vol. **69** The Media
Vol. **74** Money Matters
Vol. **75** Lone-Parent Families
Vol. **76** The Water Crisis
Vol. **77** Self-inflicted Violence
Vol. **78** Threatened Species
Vol. **79** Dealing with Homelessness
Vol. **80** The Cannabis Debate
Vol. **81** Alternative Therapies
Vol. **82** Protecting our Privacy
Vol. **83** Dealing with Crime
Vol. **84** Mental Wellbeing
Vol. **85** The Housing Crisis
Vol. **86** Smoking and your Health
Vol. **87** Genetic Modification

Vol. **88** Food and Nutrition
Vol. **89** Refugees
Vol. **90** Human and Animal Cloning
Vol. **91** Disability Issues
Vol. **92** Terrorism
Vol. **93** Binge Drinking
Vol. **94** Religions and Beliefs in Britain
Vol. **95** The Climate Crisis
Vol. **96** Preventing Sexual Diseases
Vol. **97** Energy Matters
Vol. **98** The Globalisation Issue
Vol. **99** Exploited Children
Vol. **100** Stress and Anxiety
Vol. **101** Sexuality and Discrimination
Vol. **102** The Ethics of Euthanasia
Vol. **103** Animal Rights
Vol. **104** Our Internet Society
Vol. **105** Ageing Issues
Vol. **106** Trends in Marriage
Vol. **107** Work Issues
Vol. **108** Domestic Violence

Vol. **109** Responsible Tourism
Vol. **110** Poverty
Vol. **111** The Waste Problem
Vol. **112** Women, Men and Equality
Vol. **113** Fitness and Health
Vol. **114** Drug Abuse
Vol. **115** Racial Discrimination
Vol. **116** Grief and Loss
Vol. **117** Self-Esteem and Body Image
Vol. **118** Focus on Sport
Vol. **119** Transport Trends
Vol. **120** The Human Rights Issue
Vol. **121** The Censorship Debate
Vol. **122** Bullying
Vol. **123** Young People and Health
Vol. **124** Parenting Issues
Vol. **125** Understanding Depression
Vol. **126** The Abortion Debate
Vol. **127** Eating Disorders

expenditure on health and fitness **43**.1

and homeless people **79**.15

and obesity **113**.5, 7, 10; **123**.31; **127**.32, 34

and older people **105**.3, 5, 28-39

older people and health services **105**.6, 9

and physical activity **113**.21, 22-3, 25, 29-30, 34; **118**.3, 20

and poverty **110**.6, 35

and self-esteem **117**.31, 33

students **123**.4-5

and teenage pregnancy and parenthood **75**.1, 2

and traffic pollution **119**.13-14, 31

and underweight **113**.16

and vegetarian diets **19**.15, 20, 26, 33

and walking to school **113**.39; **119**.27, 31

see also mental health; mental illness

health care

costs, obesity **127**.33-4, 37

in developing countries **20**.18

and disabled people **91**.11, 37-8, 39

and refugees **89**.19-20

healthy eating **88**.1-2, 5-7; **113**.8, 10, 32, 33; **127**.23

children **113**.4, 5, 8

as help for depression **125**.3, 39

and meat consumption **19**.4-5, 8, 10

and stress relief **100**.30, 31, 34, 35, 38-9

young people **123**.1

see also diet; food and nutrition

healthy weight maintenance *see* weight management

heart disease **113**.19-20

and alcohol consumption **93**.7, 8, 9, 18, 26, 27, 28, 30

and depression **125**.5

and exercise **113**.34

and eating disorders **127**.5

and life expectancy **105**.2, 9, 10

and meat consumption **19**.4, 15

and medical research **103**.12, 18

and milk consumption **19**.17, 18

and obesity **113**.15

and older people **105**.3

and smoking **86**.2, 3, 9-11, 13, 24-5, 31

and stress **100**.19

and vegetarians **19**.7, 8, 16, 19, 20

heatwaves, and climate change **95**.25, 27, 28

help

for alcohol problems **123**.17

for bullies **122**.2, 6-7, 8-9, 10

for depression **125**.3, 9, 13, 15, 28

for drug addiction **114**.18-19; **123**.14

for eating disorders **123**.34; **127**.25-6, 28-30

hepatitis **103**.13

and HIV **96**.10, 13

herbal cannabis (marijuana/grass) **80**.1, 4

herbal medicine **81**.4, 11, 23, 36

banned herbs **81**.24

Chinese **81**.14-15

defining **81**.2, 11

effectiveness of **81**.24

expenditure on **81**.37

and multiple sclerosis **81**.30

and pharmaceutical drugs **81**.11

regulation of **81**.23

and scientists **81**.28, 29

herbicides **87**.1, 7, 9, 10, 23, 24, 25, 29, 32

heroin

mixed with other drugs **114**.16

prices **114**.6-7

smuggling **114**.34

herpes *see* genital herpes

high blood pressure (hypertension) **19**.15; **88**.2, 9, 16

benefit of exercise **113**.34

and depression **125**.5

Hinduism **94**.6, 19, 21

and abortion and contraception **126**.2-3

beliefs **94**.2

and the Census (2001) **94**.3, 5, 28

festivals **94**.4

food rules **94**.10

funerals **116**.34

and RE (religious education) **94**.9

Hippocratic Oath **102**.1, 14

HIV (Human Immunodeficiency Virus) **96**.7, 14-39

and babies **96**.31, 39

and bacterial STIs **96**.12

and child labour **99**.3

and child soldiers **99**.31

and children **96**.20, 39; **110**.37

clinics **96**.10

defining **96**.14

in developing countries **20**.18, 20, 33

drugs and recreational drugs **114**.16

Government policies on **96**.16, 39

and 'health tourism' **96**.21, 39

and hepatitis **96**.10, 13

increase in diagnoses **96**.8, 23, 39

and parents of lesbians and gays **101**.17

and population growth **20**.5

prevention **96**.32-4

and condoms **96**.12, 14, 16, 24, 25, 29, 30, 32, 33, 34

future of **96**.34

and treatment **96**.32, 37, 38-9

prevention programmes **20**.25, 27, 28, 30, 37

and sex education **75**.21, 22, 24

and sexual behaviour **75**.16

and the sexual exploitation of children **99**.16, 24

signs and symptoms **96**.7

statistics **20**.36, 39

testing for **96**.1, 7, 8, 14, 16

transmission **96**.14, 18

treatments **96**.7, 14-15, 20-1

antiretroviral therapy (ART) **96**.36, 37, 38, 39

closing the treatment gap **96**.36-7

combination therapy **96**.15

costs of **96**.21

and prevention **96**.32, 37, 38-9

vaccines **96**.33-4

UK statistics **96**.20-2, 23

and unprotected sex **96**.12, 16, 28

and women **96**.17, 20, 24-5, 29, 30-1

pregnant **96**.16, 22, 23, 31, 38

and young people **20**.34; **96**.17, 24-9, 38

and alcohol and drug use **96**.26

education **96**.26
    young women **96**.24-5, 27-8, 29
  see also AIDS
Hodgkin's lymphoma **60**.4, 9, 10
holidays
    bookings **91**.3
    expenditure on **43**.1
    low income families **110**.5, 20
  see also responsible tourism
holism **81**.2
Holocaust denial **121**.8, 12-13
home abortions **126**.32-4
home ownership
    and debt-stress **43**.30
    house price inflation **43**.4, 8
homeless households **79**.4, 11, 19, 33; **85**.11
homeless young people **79**.4, 11, 20-1, 23-5
homelessness
    and affordable housing **79**.1, 2, 9, 11-12, 35
    and beggars **79**.26, 34-5
    and children **79**.4, 8
    defining **79**.10
    and domestic violence **79**.13, 37
    effects of **79**.12
    and health **79**.15, 39
    the 'hidden homeless' **79**.10, 39
    and human rights **79**.32
    and the law **79**.8, 30
    and mental health problems **79**.2, 10, 15, 16-17, 19, 32
    and missing persons **79**.13-14
    and older people **79**.9
    public attitudes to **79**.4, 32
    reasons for **79**.1, 2, 4, 10-11, 12, 18, 20-1
    research into **79**.3, 5-7, 17, 39
    and the 'revolving door' syndrome **79**.32, 33-4
    statistics **79**.10, 19, 32, 36
    stereotypes of homeless people **79**.20, 21
    tackling **79**.27-39
  see also homeless young people; rough sleepers; single
    homelessness
homeopathy **81**.12-13, 23, 36
    and cancer **81**.32

defining **81**.2, 12
effectiveness of **81**.22, 24, 28
expenditure on **81**.37
and the placebo effect **81**.26
and scientists **81**.28-9
treatments **81**.12-13
homeworking **107**.12, 14-15, 19-20, 22
homicide
    and domestic violence **108**.7
    and guns **83**.4
    increase in rates of **83**.3
homophobia
    in football **118**.17
    hate crime **101**.29, 36-7
    homophobic bullying **101**.3, 13, 18, 19, 20, 21-2, 38-9;
      122.3
    and male friendships **112**.34
    and mental health problems **101**.20
homosexuality
    acceptability of **112**.38
    and ageing **101**.9
    awareness of **101**.14-15
    and Christianity **101**.5-7, 15, 18, 29
    coming out **101**.11-13
      in the workplace **101**.23-4
    'correction' of **101**.5-6, 10
    equality struggles **101**.9
    and genes **101**.8, 14
    and the law **101**.3, 10
    same-sex partnerships and the law **101**.30-2
    and section 28 of the Local Government Bill **101**.28-9
      repeal of **101**.18, 21, 22, 29, 39
    and young people **123**.21
hooliganism, football **118**.7, 8
honour crimes **108**.24
hormonal methods of contraception **123**.23
  see also pill, contraceptive
hormones
    and appetite regulation **127**.38-9
    use in sport **118**.37
horse racing
    age restrictions on gambling **29**.2

Volume numbers appear first (in bold) followed by page numbers; a change in volume number is preceded by a semi-colon.

Vol. **19** Looking at Vegetarianism
Vol. **20** Population Growth
Vol. **22** Confronting Child Abuse
Vol. **29** Gambling
Vol. **43** A Consumer Society
Vol. **60** Confronting Cancer
Vol. **69** The Media
Vol. **74** Money Matters
Vol. **75** Lone-Parent Families
Vol. **76** The Water Crisis
Vol. **77** Self-inflicted Violence
Vol. **78** Threatened Species
Vol. **79** Dealing with Homelessness
Vol. **80** The Cannabis Debate
Vol. **81** Alternative Therapies
Vol. **82** Protecting our Privacy
Vol. **83** Dealing with Crime
Vol. **84** Mental Wellbeing
Vol. **85** The Housing Crisis
Vol. **86** Smoking and your Health
Vol. **87** Genetic Modification

Vol. **88** Food and Nutrition
Vol. **89** Refugees
Vol. **90** Human and Animal Cloning
Vol. **91** Disability Issues
Vol. **92** Terrorism
Vol. **93** Binge Drinking
Vol. **94** Religions and Beliefs in Britain
Vol. **95** The Climate Crisis
Vol. **96** Preventing Sexual Diseases
Vol. **97** Energy Matters
Vol. **98** The Globalisation Issue
Vol. **99** Exploited Children
Vol. **100** Stress and Anxiety
Vol. **101** Sexuality and Discrimination
Vol. **102** The Ethics of Euthanasia
Vol. **103** Animal Rights
Vol. **104** Our Internet Society
Vol. **105** Ageing Issues
Vol. **106** Trends in Marriage
Vol. **107** Work Issues
Vol. **108** Domestic Violence

Vol. **109** Responsible Tourism
Vol. **110** Poverty
Vol. **111** The Waste Problem
Vol. **112** Women, Men and Equality
Vol. **113** Fitness and Health
Vol. **114** Drug Abuse
Vol. **115** Racial Discrimination
Vol. **116** Grief and Loss
Vol. **117** Self-Esteem and Body Image
Vol. **118** Focus on Sport
Vol. **119** Transport Trends
Vol. **120** The Human Rights Issue
Vol. **121** The Censorship Debate
Vol. **122** Bullying
Vol. **123** Young People and Health
Vol. **124** Parenting Issues
Vol. **125** Understanding Depression
Vol. **126** The Abortion Debate
Vol. **127** Eating Disorders

expenditure on **29**.9
percentage of people participating **29**.7
hospice care **60**.8, 13; **102**.3-4, 13, 28, 31
hospitality industry **86**.17, 19, 20-3
hospitals
    admission for manic depression **125**.19-20
    and cases of self-harm **77**.6, 9, 10, 29
    and mental illness **84**.10, 36
hostels **79**.32-4
hours of work **107**.2, 3, 6, 14, 24
    fathers **124**.11
    full-time mothers **124**.12
    inequality **110**.14
    see also employment
house prices **85**.1, 3-4
    and first-time buyers **85**.6, 7
    regional differences in **85**.3-4, 6, 8
    and single people **85**.7
household tasks and working parents **124**.11
household waste **111**.3
    composition of **111**.22
    food packaging **111**.11
    kerbside collections of **111**.3, 29
    microchip analysis **111**.38
    prevention **111**.16
    recycling **111**.6
    see also composting waste; waste management
households
    average size of **43**.2
    and energy efficiency **95**.29, 30-1; **97**.2, 27-30, 31, 32-3
    expenditure patterns **43**.1, 2, 3-4
        gap between rich and poor **43**.13
        and older people **105**.5
    growth in numbers of **85**.1-2, 3, 29
        and the need for new homes **85**.8-9, 20
    income gap **110**.16
    low income **110**.12-13
    number of single-person **75**.29
    size of **106**.2, 3
    structure and child poverty **110**.12-13
    weekly expenditure **43**.13
    see also families; homeless households
housework
    and men **112**.30
    parents, time spent on **124**.11
housing
    and child poverty **110**.12
    costs **79**.9
    and the environment **85**.14-15, 26
    expenditure on **79**.9
    home ownership in the UK **85**.30
    housing crisis 'backlog' **85**.2
    in London **85**.10-13, 16-17
    and lone parents **75**.38
    need for new homes **85**.1-3, 8-9
        numbers required **85**.9, 20
        and planning laws **85**.20
        targets **85**.1
    new house-building
        in cities **85**.25
        and housing density **85**.25, 34

    in the M11 region **85**.18, 22, 26, 27, 33
    numbers being built **85**.3
    and planning permission **85**.35
    in the Thames Gateway **85**.21-4, 26, 33
    and older people **105**.6
    and overcrowded accommodation **79**.1
    poverty and poor housing conditions **79**.9
    and same-sex partnerships **101**.31
    and sex discrimination **112**.14
    size of houses in the UK **85**.30
    and teenage parenthood **75**.2
    and urban growth in developing countries **20**.17-18
    see also affordable housing; homelessness; rural housing;
        temporary accommodation
housing benefit **79**.9, 12, 36
HTML (Hypertext Markup Language) **104**.2
human reproductive cloning **90**.1-25
    arguments against **90**.1, 24
    arguments for **90**.1, 3-4
    autonomy issues **90**.4
    bans on **90**.10, 11, 14, 22, 25, 33
    behavioural similarities to donors **90**.8, 12, 20
    biological age **90**.9
    cloning for birth **90**.6-7
    definition of a clone **90**.2
    and dignity **90**.4, 5
    ethical standards **90**.3, 4, 12, 15, 18, 19, 22
    and gay couple reproduction **90**.21
    and gene therapy **90**.11
    health of cloned humans **90**.1, 2, 3, 7, 9
        psychological/social health **90**.4, 12
    and infertility treatments **90**.11
    licences for embryo research **90**.23
    mixing human cells and animal eggs **90**.19
    and motherhood **90**.8-9
    religious opinion on **90**.22
    research standards **90**.3-4
    spare part organs **90**.20
    and super-human people **90**.20-1
    uses for **90**.3
human rights **98**.29, 38; **120**.23-7
    and animal rights **103**.33
    and CCTV **82**.24
    and child labour **99**.4, 6
        domestic work **99**.8
    and child protection **22**.25-6
    and child soldiers **99**.30, 31-2
    and children's rights **120**.1-22
    and euthanasia **102**.13
    and homelessness **79**.32
    and identity cards **120**.37
    and privacy **82**.4-5, 18
    and refugees **120**.31
    and surveillance **120**.33
    and terrorism **92**.25
    water as a human right **76**.24-5, 32
    and workers **120**.28-31
humanism
    and abortion **126**.4-5
    and euthanasia **102**.1-2
    and faith-based projects **94**.16

and faith-based schools **94**.31

funerals **116**.35

and the Golden Rule **94**.11

and 'incitement to religious hatred' **94**.32

and the law on freedom of religion or belief **94**.29

and RE (religious education) **94**.9, 15

and religious diversity **94**.38-9

hunger

developing world **110**.31-2

eradication **87**.28-30, 33, 36

Millennium Development Goals **110**.30-31

hunting **103**.24-31

arguments against **103**.26

arguments for **103**.24-5

before the ban **103**.26

and the control of wild animals **103**.25

and cruelty **103**.25, 26

deer hunting **103**.24, 28

draghunting **103**.24-5, 26

fox numbers and the ban on **103**.26

and Globally Threatened Birds **78**.8

hare coursing **103**.25, 26, 27

history of the abolition of **103**.27-8

and hounds **103**.24

hunt saboteurs **103**.28, 30

law on (Hunting Act 2004) **103**.26, 27

testing enforcement of **103**.31

public attitudes to **103**.24, 25-

whales **78**.6, 13, 14

of wildlife **78**.2, 4-5, 5-6

hybrid vehicles **119**.22

hydrocarbon (HC) emissions **119**.15

ice sheets

melting **95**.3, 5, 8, 12-15, 24, 33, 39

ICT (Information and Communication Technologies)

and online learning **104**.9-10, 11

identical people **90**.1, 2, 3, 20

identity

British identity of non-white ethnic groups **115**.38

racial, victims of crime **115**.10

religious **115**.5, 26

identity (ID) cards **82**.1, 2, 7-12; **120**.34, 35-6

and biometric data **82**.9, 10, 12

and bogus asylum seekers **82**.7, 8

and civil liberties **82**.11-12

and electronic fraud **82**.11

fee to be charged for **82**.7, 8, 10

fraud **82**.7, 8

and health and welfare benefit abuse **82**.7, 8, 9

and human rights **120**.37

and identity fraud **82**.11, 12

opposition to **82**.7, 8

and personal freedom **82**.8

public attitudes to **82**.7-8

illegal drugs trade **114**.33-5

illegal dumping *see* fly-tipping

illegal employment **89**.10-11, 30-1

illegal immigrants **89**.11, 30-1

illness and depression **125**.2, 5-6

immigration

illegal immigrants **89**.11, 30-1

and population growth **20**.4-5, 11, 15-16, 32

see also asylum seekers; ethnic minorities

immunisation

and animal diseases **103**.12

and life expectancy **105**.2

imports **98**.1, 9

in vitro (in glass) research **103**.14, 18, 19

inactivity

children **113**.7, 8

and coronary heart disease **113**.20

incentives for recycling **111**.34, 37

incineration **111**.3, 6, 22

disadvantages **111**.7, 15, 22

inclusion

and behavioural problems in schools **120**.16

concept **91**.29-30, 30, 32

and sport **118**.12

disabled people **118**.22

Volume numbers appear first (in bold) followed by page numbers; a change in volume number is preceded by a semi-colon.

Vol. **19** Looking at Vegetarianism
Vol. **20** Population Growth
Vol. **22** Confronting Child Abuse
Vol. **29** Gambling
Vol. **43** A Consumer Society
Vol. **60** Confronting Cancer
Vol. **69** The Media
Vol. **74** Money Matters
Vol. **75** Lone-Parent Families
Vol. **76** The Water Crisis
Vol. **77** Self-inflicted Violence
Vol. **78** Threatened Species
Vol. **79** Dealing with Homelessness
Vol. **80** The Cannabis Debate
Vol. **81** Alternative Therapies
Vol. **82** Protecting our Privacy
Vol. **83** Dealing with Crime
Vol. **84** Mental Wellbeing
Vol. **85** The Housing Crisis
Vol. **86** Smoking and your Health
Vol. **87** Genetic Modification

Vol. **88** Food and Nutrition
Vol. **89** Refugees
Vol. **90** Human and Animal Cloning
Vol. **91** Disability Issues
Vol. **92** Terrorism
Vol. **93** Binge Drinking
Vol. **94** Religions and Beliefs in Britain
Vol. **95** The Climate Crisis
Vol. **96** Preventing Sexual Diseases
Vol. **97** Energy Matters
Vol. **98** The Globalisation Issue
Vol. **99** Exploited Children
Vol. **100** Stress and Anxiety
Vol. **101** Sexuality and Discrimination
Vol. **102** The Ethics of Euthanasia
Vol. **103** Animal Rights
Vol. **104** Our Internet Society
Vol. **105** Ageing Issues
Vol. **106** Trends in Marriage
Vol. **107** Work Issues
Vol. **108** Domestic Violence

Vol. **109** Responsible Tourism
Vol. **110** Poverty
Vol. **111** The Waste Problem
Vol. **112** Women, Men and Equality
Vol. **113** Fitness and Health
Vol. **114** Drug Abuse
Vol. **115** Racial Discrimination
Vol. **116** Grief and Loss
Vol. **117** Self-Esteem and Body Image
Vol. **118** Focus on Sport
Vol. **119** Transport Trends
Vol. **120** The Human Rights Issue
Vol. **121** The Censorship Debate
Vol. **122** Bullying
Vol. **123** Young People and Health
Vol. **124** Parenting Issues
Vol. **125** Understanding Depression
Vol. **126** The Abortion Debate
Vol. **127** Eating Disorders

ethnic minorities **118**.13-16
    women **118**.18-22
incomes **98**.5, 13, 18, 32, 33; **107**.2, 13
    inequality of **43**.4, 13
        global **110**.35
        UK **110**.13, 14, 16
    minimum wage **43**.4; **75**.10; **107**.31
    older people **105**.4-5
    and older women **105**.21
    and part-time working **107**.17
    single-parent families **124**.35
    stress and income levels **100**.13
    women **110**.17-18
    young people **110**.10
    see also equal pay; wages
indirect euthanasia **102**.1
indirect racial discrimination **115**.7, 11
indirect sex discrimination **112**.13
industrial waste disposal **111**.24
industrialisation
    and climate change **95**.3, 9
    and population growth **20**.2
industry
    and child labour **99**.1, 2
    and energy efficiency **95**.34
    water consumption **76**.2, 8, 36
    water pollution **76**.11
inequality
    gender *see* gender gap
    and globalisation **98**.5, 13, 33-4
    of incomes **43**.4, 13; **110**.13, 14, 16, 35
    and segregation **115**.30, 31, 32
    and terrorism **92**.13, 21
    see also child poverty; poverty
infant mortality **20**.28, 29, 30, 31
infections
    as cause of anorexia **127**.12
    as cause of depression **125**.5
infertility **86**.25
    and anti-abortion movement **126**.25
information technology (IT)
    educational projects **82**.28
    and globalisation **98**.4
    see also computers
inquests **116**.32
    and suicide **77**.1, 36-7
insecticides **87**.7, 19, 23, 24, 25, 29
insomnia
    and stress **100**.19, 29
instant messaging (IM) and bullying **122**.20, 21
insurance
    car insurance offences **119**.9
    and homeworking **107**.20
    life insurance **106**.14
    and money management **106**.14
    and privacy rights **82**.25-6
    and sustainable tourism **109**.28
    and young people **74**.2, 15
    and young travellers **109**.11, 12, 13, 14-15
integrated medicine/healthcare **81**.36-8
intellectual property rights **87**.29, 32; **98**.21, 22

inter-ethnic marriages **115**.25
    see also mixed-race relationships
interest rates
    and consumer spending **43**.1, 8
    credit card **43**.28; **74**.26, 27
    and mortgage repayments **85**.6
    and savings **74**.24
interests, and improving self-esteem **117**.6, 8, 33
internally displaced persons **89**.1, 6, 8-9
international anti-doping policy **118**.27-8, 31-2
international law and child labour **120**.20
international trade **98**.4, 21-3
    and poverty **110**.22, 30
    see also globalisation
Internet
    access **69**.1, 3
    addiction **104**.36-7
    banking **74**.2; **104**.12
    banning children from using **22**.22
    and British consumers **43**.10
    broadband access **104**.3, 12
    bullying by e-mail **122**.5, 19, 21
    and censorship **121**.18-21
        China **121**.2, 19-20
    and children and young people **104**.3-5, 9-11
        access **104**.3, 13
        and chat rooms **104**.5, 20-1
        nature of use **104**.3-4
        online communication **104**.4-5
        online learning **104**.9-10, 11
        and parents **104**.4, 9-10
        and safety **104**.17-29
        statistics **104**.3-5
    file sharing **104**.39
    fraud **43**.26, 28, 39-40
    household access **43**.3
    instant messaging **104**.35
    movie-swapping **104**.38-9
    non-users **104**.15
    and older people **105**.8, 11
    online bullying **122**.19-26
    online gambling **29**.3, 4, 7, 10-15, 23
    online shopping
        addiction to **43**.38-9
        and young people **43**.23-4
    and paedophiles
        'anti-grooming' orders **22**.38, 39
        and chatrooms **22**.32, 33, 35, 38-9
    phishing **104**.32-3
    and the sexual exploitation of children **99**.16, 21, 24
    shopping **104**.5-8
    surveillance
        and the Government **82**.1, 22, 23
        in the workplace **82**.25, 26, 27, 28; **120**.32
    see also child pornography; e-mail; safety and the Internet; websites
Internet Service Providers (ISPs) **104**.1
    and child pornography websites **104**.29
    and spam **104**.30, 31
intersexuality **101**.7
involuntary euthanasia **102**.1

IRA (Irish Republican Army) **92**.2, 11, 23; **94**.10
iridology **81**.17-18
iris recognition, and identity cards **82**.9, 10, 11, 12
iron in the diet **19**.3, 5, 8; **88**.6, 15
   teenagers' needs **123**.6
irrigation **87**.35
   and global water supplies **76**.3, 4, 5, 19
   and water shortages **76**.21
Islam
   and abortion and contraception **126**.2
   and the Census (2001) **94**.3, 5, 28
   festivals **94**.4, 35, 36
   five pillars of **94**.3-4
   food rules **94**.10
   funerals **116**.34-5
   Golden Rule **94**.8, 11
   and 'honour killings' **94**.30
   media treatment of **94**.33
   Muslim schools **94**.12, 13, 14
   new religious movements/cults **94**.19, 21, 25
   and RE (religious education) **94**.9, 31
   and terrorism **92**.13
      condemnation of **92**.26, 28-9, 37-8
      convictions of Muslims in the UK **92**.27
   tradition and beliefs **94**.2
Islamophobia **115**.36
IVF (in vitro fertilisation) **90**.12, 19

J

Jainism **94**.2
Jehovah's Witnesses **94**.1, 19
Jews
   and abortion and contraception **126**.3
   beliefs **94**.2, 4
   and the Census (2001) **94**.3, 5, 28
   festivals **94**.4
   food rules **94**.10
   funerals **116**.33-4
   Jewish schools **94**.30

   and racism laws **115**.26
   and RE (religious education) **94**.9
   terrorist groups **92**.2-3
job hunting **107**.31-2
job prospects and obesity **113**.17
job satisfaction **107**.1-2, 13
   women **112**.22-3
job security **98**.5; **107**.1, 2
journey length trends **119**.29
   travelling to school **119**.30
junk food advertising, effect on childhood obesity **113**.2
junk mail **111**.5
justice system and children **120**.12

K

ketamine **114**.3, 31
   and drug mixing **114**.17
   and drugs market **114**.6
kerbside recycling **111**.3, 29
key workers
   affordable housing for **85**.1, 3, 20
      in the Thames Gateway **85**.21, 22, 23
   see also public sector workers
khat and the law **114**.31-2
kidney cancer **60**.5, 16, 17
   in childhood **60**.9, 11
kidney damage and eating disorders **127**.5
kinesiology **81**.2
kitchen waste **111**.31, 33

L

labour costs **98**.13
labour market
   and tourism **109**.32
   and women **112**.12

Volume numbers appear first (in bold) followed by page numbers; a change in volume number is preceded by a semi-colon.

Vol. **19** Looking at Vegetarianism	Vol. **88** Food and Nutrition	Vol. **109** Responsible Tourism
Vol. **20** Population Growth	Vol. **89** Refugees	Vol. **110** Poverty
Vol. **22** Confronting Child Abuse	Vol. **90** Human and Animal Cloning	Vol. **111** The Waste Problem
Vol. **29** Gambling	Vol. **91** Disability Issues	Vol. **112** Women, Men and Equality
Vol. **43** A Consumer Society	Vol. **92** Terrorism	Vol. **113** Fitness and Health
Vol. **60** Confronting Cancer	Vol. **93** Binge Drinking	Vol. **114** Drug Abuse
Vol. **69** The Media	Vol. **94** Religions and Beliefs in Britain	Vol. **115** Racial Discrimination
Vol. **74** Money Matters	Vol. **95** The Climate Crisis	Vol. **116** Grief and Loss
Vol. **75** Lone-Parent Families	Vol. **96** Preventing Sexual Diseases	Vol. **117** Self-Esteem and Body Image
Vol. **76** The Water Crisis	Vol. **97** Energy Matters	Vol. **118** Focus on Sport
Vol. **77** Self-inflicted Violence	Vol. **98** The Globalisation Issue	Vol. **119** Transport Trends
Vol. **78** Threatened Species	Vol. **99** Exploited Children	Vol. **120** The Human Rights Issue
Vol. **79** Dealing with Homelessness	Vol. **100** Stress and Anxiety	Vol. **121** The Censorship Debate
Vol. **80** The Cannabis Debate	Vol. **101** Sexuality and Discrimination	Vol. **122** Bullying
Vol. **81** Alternative Therapies	Vol. **102** The Ethics of Euthanasia	Vol. **123** Young People and Health
Vol. **82** Protecting our Privacy	Vol. **103** Animal Rights	Vol. **124** Parenting Issues
Vol. **83** Dealing with Crime	Vol. **104** Our Internet Society	Vol. **125** Understanding Depression
Vol. **84** Mental Wellbeing	Vol. **105** Ageing Issues	Vol. **126** The Abortion Debate
Vol. **85** The Housing Crisis	Vol. **106** Trends in Marriage	Vol. **127** Eating Disorders
Vol. **86** Smoking and your Health	Vol. **107** Work Issues	
Vol. **87** Genetic Modification	Vol. **108** Domestic Violence	

working conditions in the tourist industry **109**.30, 31, 32

lacto-ovo-vegetarians **19**.1, 6

lacto-vegetarians **19**.1

landfill **111**.3, 5, 6, 22
  problems **111**.7, 15, 22
  tax **111**.3, 7

language
  barriers to employment **89**.27, 35, 37
  in schools and gender equality **112**.10
  strong language on television **121**.38-9

Large Offspring Syndrome **90**.27-8, 35

laughter as help in grieving **116**.13

law *see* legislation

Lawrence Report (Macpherson Inquiry) **115**.8

laxatives, effects **127**.2

leachate **111**.3, 15

leadership skills development, women **112**.15-16

leakage, and the tourist industry **109**.32-3

learning disabilities **91**.26-39
  autistic spectrum disorders **91**.26, 28
  and bullying **91**.26
  causes of **91**.26, 27
  children with **91**.28, 29-30
  definition **91**.26, 27
  diagnosing **91**.27
  and health care **91**.37-8, 39
  inclusion concept **91**.30, 32
  and mental health **84**.2; **91**.4, 26
  number of people with **91**.26, 29
  special needs education **91**.7, 10, 29-36
  types of **91**.27
  see also disabled people

legal rights, young people **120**.7-8

legislation **91**.17
  and abortion **126**.5, 6, 7-8, 12
  and alcohol **123**.16
  on asylum **89**.3-4, 11, 12, 33, 39
  and bullying **122**.11
    racist bullying **122**.4
  and drugs *see* drugs and the law
  on embryo research **90**.13, 15, 33
  and film classification **121**.23-5
  on food additives **88**.39
  on food labelling **88**.23, 24, 25
  on littering **111**.9, 19
  protection from domestic violence **108**.38-9
  and racism **115**.2, 7-8, 26
    at work **115**.11-12
  on religious hatred **115**.26; **121**.7, 15
  and smoking, young people **123**.12
  and video **121**.31
  on waste treatment **111**.2

leisure
  expenditure on **43**.1, 13
  and older people **105**.5, 28

lesbians
  and bullying in schools **101**.19
  and homophobic bullying **101**.3
  issues facing young women **101**.19-20
  and the law **101**.3, 10, 27, 28
  and sexually transmitted infections **101**.4
  and workplace discrimination **101**.23, 24
  see also gay couples; homosexuality

leukaemia **60**.5, 9, 16, 17, 33
  bone marrow transplants for **60**.35
  childhood **60**.9, 10, 12
  and medical research **103**.12

liability for racism at work **115**.12

liberalisation **98**.2-3, 9, 23

life expectancy **98**.12
  and AIDS **20**.3, 5, 11
  and alcohol consumption **93**.9
  in developed regions **20**.5
  and gender **105**.2, 9-10
  increase in **105**.35
    reasons for **105**.1-2
  in less developed regions **20**.5, 18
  and smoking **86**.31
  ways of increasing **105**.29-31

lifestyle
  and life expectancy **105**.2, 9-10, 36
  and obesity **113**.6, 7, 9
    in children **113**.1, 2
  and older people **105**.34
  sedentary lifestyles, children **113**.1, 7, 8
  sports **118**.1
  stress and changes in **100**.19

lip cancer **60**.5

listening as help for bereaved **116**.14-15

listeria **88**.28-9

litter **111**.3, 8-10, 19
  bins **111**.9
  campaigns **111**.8
  as criminal offence **111**.19
  legal definition **111**.9

liver cancer **60**.5, 9, 16, 17

liver disease and alcohol consumption **93**.7, 8, 11, 18, 28, 33, 37

living alone
  lesbian, gay and bisexual people **101**.9
  numbers of people **85**.2
  single men **106**.12

living standards **98**.12
  and water consumption **76**.8

living wills *see* advance directives (living wills)

loans *see* credit

local authorities and litter **111**.8, 19

local communities **98**.38
  and tourist development **109**.32

local economy, and tourism **109**.31

lone parents **20**.26, 33; **75**.28-39; **124**.33-5
  and childcare **75**.30, 38, 39
  children of **75**.28, 29; **124**.22, 33-4
  and daughters of teenage mothers **75**.2
  and divorce **75**.28, 31, 33, 35; **124**.33-4
    money matters **75**.38
  and employment **75**.30
    finding work **112**.12
    in full-time work **75**.37-8
    starting work **75**.39
  fathers **75**.28, 34-6

financial management **75**.37-8, 39
and household income **75**.31
and housing **75**.38
marital status **75**.28, 31, 32
myths about **75**.28, 32, 33
never-married **75**.28, 31, 32
and poverty **75**.31, 32, 39; **110**.12-13, 17
and State benefits **75**.31, 38
statistics **75**.28, 29, 31, 32; **106**.2, 3; **124**.35
teenage **126**.31
see also teenage pregnancies
loneliness
feelings after bereavement **116**.4, 19
and older people **105**.12
long-term poverty **110**.1, 6, 13
loss on childhood, and low self-esteem **117**.32
low carbon technologies **97**.4
low self-esteem (LSE) **117**.5-8, 31
and bullying **122**.8
causes of **117**.31-2
and eating disorders **127**.2
LPG vehicles **119**.20
LSD, mixed with other drugs **114**.16

M

macro-terrorism **92**.11
macrobiotic diets **19**.1
magazines
advertising in **69**.14, 28-9, 33
influence on body image **117**.11-12, 15
readership **69**.28-9
UK market in **69**.24, 28
magic mushrooms **114**.32, 35
magnetic field therapy **81**.30, 31
mail order fraud **43**.26, 35
maize (GM) **87**.4, 8, 9, 12, 13, 27, 31, 32
malaria **76**.6
and climate change **95**.7, 9, 12, 15, 17, 39
malnutrition *see* hunger

managers
management style and workplace bullying **122**.29, 35
women **112**.18
and workplace stress **100**.18, 25
manic depression *see* bipolar affective disorder
manufactured goods **91**.13; **98**.10
manufacturing sector employment **107**.7, 10
marijuana **114**.4
marital status
and population in England and Wales **106**.26
and remarriages **106**.32
marriage
age at **106**.3, 25
as an institution **106**.5-6
as a relationship **106**.5-6
arranged marriages **106**.15, 15-18; **108**.24
attitudes to **106**.4-6, 11
births outside **124**.22
changing views on **106**.4-6, 20
and Civil Partnerships **101**.33-4
'common law' marriages **106**.8, 9-10
early and forced marriage **120**.29
forced marriages abroad **106**.15
Government policies on **106**.31
and HIV/AIDS **96**.24-5, 29, 34, 35
inter-ethnic **115**.25
and life expectancy **105**.30
male and female attitudes to **106**.6
open marriages **106**.18-19
and premarital contracts **106**.22-4
and rape **108**.6
remarriages **106**.2, 3, 32
statistics **106**.2, 3
and tax incentives **106**.26
marriage counselling **106**.27
martyrdom, and suicide attacks **92**.16
masculinity **112**.33-4
and gender equality **112**.36-8
and health risks **112**.37
rules of **112**.36
and violence **112**.37-8
massage **81**.4

Volume numbers appear first (in bold) followed by page numbers; a change in volume number is preceded by a semi-colon.

Vol. **19** Looking at Vegetarianism
Vol. **20** Population Growth
Vol. **22** Confronting Child Abuse
Vol. **29** Gambling
Vol. **43** A Consumer Society
Vol. **60** Confronting Cancer
Vol. **69** The Media
Vol. **74** Money Matters
Vol. **75** Lone-Parent Families
Vol. **76** The Water Crisis
Vol. **77** Self-inflicted Violence
Vol. **78** Threatened Species
Vol. **79** Dealing with Homelessness
Vol. **80** The Cannabis Debate
Vol. **81** Alternative Therapies
Vol. **82** Protecting our Privacy
Vol. **83** Dealing with Crime
Vol. **84** Mental Wellbeing
Vol. **85** The Housing Crisis
Vol. **86** Smoking and your Health
Vol. **87** Genetic Modification

Vol. **88** Food and Nutrition
Vol. **89** Refugees
Vol. **90** Human and Animal Cloning
Vol. **91** Disability Issues
Vol. **92** Terrorism
Vol. **93** Binge Drinking
Vol. **94** Religions and Beliefs in Britain
Vol. **95** The Climate Crisis
Vol. **96** Preventing Sexual Diseases
Vol. **97** Energy Matters
Vol. **98** The Globalisation Issue
Vol. **99** Exploited Children
Vol. **100** Stress and Anxiety
Vol. **101** Sexuality and Discrimination
Vol. **102** The Ethics of Euthanasia
Vol. **103** Animal Rights
Vol. **104** Our Internet Society
Vol. **105** Ageing Issues
Vol. **106** Trends in Marriage
Vol. **107** Work Issues
Vol. **108** Domestic Violence

Vol. **109** Responsible Tourism
Vol. **110** Poverty
Vol. **111** The Waste Problem
Vol. **112** Women, Men and Equality
Vol. **113** Fitness and Health
Vol. **114** Drug Abuse
Vol. **115** Racial Discrimination
Vol. **116** Grief and Loss
Vol. **117** Self-Esteem and Body Image
Vol. **118** Focus on Sport
Vol. **119** Transport Trends
Vol. **120** The Human Rights Issue
Vol. **121** The Censorship Debate
Vol. **122** Bullying
Vol. **123** Young People and Health
Vol. **124** Parenting Issues
Vol. **125** Understanding Depression
Vol. **126** The Abortion Debate
Vol. **127** Eating Disorders

and raising self-esteem **117**.33
see also aromatherapy
materials reclamation facility (MRF) **111**.3, 6
maternal mortality, global **112**.39
maternity leave **107**.16, 21
maximum working hours **107**.30-1
means tested benefits **110**.18
meat consumption **88**.6, 26, 31
    cooking meat **19**.8, 10
    and fat **19**.10
    and healthy eating **19**.3, 4-5, 8, 10
    and iron **19**.5
    meat-based diets **19**.15
media
    and attitudes to teenage sexuality **75**.3
    and body image **117**.11-12, 15, 17-18; **127**.23
      and eating disorders **127**.25-6, 27
    breaking ethnic stereotypes **115**.22
    coverage of mental health issues **84**.21, 22
    coverage of terrorism **92**.10, 23-4, 27, 28-9, 37
    government control **121**.1
    government use of **121**.17-18
    and the law **69**.31, 34, 35, 38-9
    ownership **121**.4-5
    portrayals of lesbians and gays **101**.15
    and the reporting of suicides **77**.16, 20, 37
    social effects of **69**.1-15
    teenage magazines **69**.33
    UK media ownership **69**.22-5
    violence *see* violence, media
    and women's sport **118**.21-2
    see also films; newspapers; television
mediation, and divorce **106**.38-9
medical abortion ('the abortion pill') **126**.10, 14, 32-4
medical model of disability **91**.6, 29
medical technology
    and advance directives **102**.36-7
    and animal experiments **103**.10-11
    and euthanasia **102**.1, 3, 29, 30, 31
medical treatment
    withdrawal of, and the law **102**.3
medicinal use of cannabis **80**.5, 7, 12, 22, 34, 35-9; **114**.39
    as an anti-emetic **80**.37
    as an appetite stimulant **80**.37
    and cannabinoids **80**.38
    and cannabis reclassification **80**.34
    GW Pharmaceuticals trials **80**.26, 35, 37, 38-9
    legality of **80**.38-9
    and multiple sclerosis (MS) **80**.35
    as a painkiller **80**.22, 26, 37
    public attitudes to **80**.36
    safety of **80**.38
    and terminal illnesses **80**.37
medicines
    animal testing of **103**.1, 11, 12-14
      drug development **103**.2-3, 9, 10, 11, 13
    and banned substances in sport **118**.32-3
    and older people **105**.38-9
melanoma (skin cancer) **60**.5, 18, 19-21
memorial services **116**.17

men
    and abortion
      involvement in decision-making **126**.13, 15-16
      rights **126**.15
    and alcohol
      binge drinking **93**.1, 2, 36
      and hospital admissions **93**.9
      safe limits **93**.2, 3, 4, 27, 29, 38
    body image and the media **117**.12
    and cancer **60**.3, 4, 5
      breast cancer **60**.22
      lung cancer **60**.4, 15, 26
      prostate cancer **60**.3, 4, 6, 13, 24-5, 35
      testicular cancer **60**.5, 18, 26
    and child abuse **22**.1, 3, 4, 6, 10
    childcare careers **112**.23-4
    and condom use **75**.15, 16
    and debt problems **43**.30
    and depression **125**.13-15
    and divorce **106**.31
    and eating disorders **127**.3
    and gambling **29**.8, 26
    and gender equality **112**.36-8
    and gender identity **112**.36
    and higher education **112**.1, 8
    life expectancy **105**.2, 9, 19
    and mental illness **84**.1
    older men and employment **105**.21, 22
    and self-harm **77**.14
    and sexual abuse **22**.15
    and sexual health **96**.13
    single **106**.3, 12, 20
    and stress **100**.13, 19
    and suicide **77**.2; **84**.1
    see also boys and young men; fathers; gay men; infertility; masculinity
meningitis **123**.5
mental health
    and abortion **126**.11
    and adolescents **123**.9
    and alcohol consumption **93**.28
    benefits of exercise **113**.22
    and cannabis **80**.7, 10, 12, 13, 14, 16, 19-20, 26; **114**.37, 38
    costs of mental health care **84**.1, 38
    and diet **125**.11-12
    education in **84**.4, 30-2
    and homophobia **101**.20
    and older people **105**.3, 37-9
    and self-harm **77**.6-7, 8, 10, 11, 13
    statistics **84**.1, 20; **125**.16
    and suicide **77**.3
      and parents **77**.36
      and public policy **77**.17-18
      and students **77**.15, 22, 23
    and workplace stress **100**.17-18, 20
    see also dementia; depression
mental illness
    attitudes to **84**.4-5, 21-2
      challenging the stigma of **84**.19-20, 25-6
    breakdowns **84**.4-5

and cannabis **114**.37, 38
causes of **84**.9
characteristics of **84**.2-3
defining **84**.8, 22
and eating disorders **127**.9-10
genetic predisposition to **84**.5
help for people with **84**.10
and homelessness **79**.2, 10, 15, 16-17, 19, 32
and learning disabilities **84**.2
likelihood of suffering from **84**.4
myths about **84**.23, 26
recovery from **84**.5
and students **84**.32-3
symptoms of **84**.8-9, 20
treatment **84**.25, 27
    depression **84**.35-6
    future of **84**.26
types of **84**.1
and violence **84**.4, 18
and young people **84**.1, 5-6, 8-10, 13-15, 28, 30-2
see also depression; schizophrenia
mental symptoms of workplace bullying **122**.31
mental toughness and resisting bullying **122**.38
metals recycling **111**.23, 31, 36
aluminium **111**.11, 23-4, 26
methane
    and global warming **95**.1, 4, 5, 6, 9
    produced from landfill **111**.3, 15
Methodist Church **94**.1, 19
microbes **88**.27, 28-9
microbicides **96**.34, 35
Mifepristone (the abortion pill) **126**.10, 14, 32-4
migrant worker exploitation **120**.30-31
migration **98**.2
    and climate change **95**.7, 12, 15, 17
    and population growth **20**.4-5, 6, 11
        in the UK **85**.29, 30
    see also asylum seekers
minimum wage **43**.4; **107**.31
miscegenation *see* mixed-race relationships
missing persons **79**.13-14
mixed-faith relationships **115**.39

mixed-race families **124**.36-7
mixed-race people, Britain **115**.24-5
    as victims of crime **115**.10
mixed-race relationships **115**.22-3, 24-5
MNCs (multi-national corporations) **98**.3, 25
mobile phones
    bullying by **122**.19, 21-5
    and the elderly **105**.10-11
    and the Internet **104**.4-5
    market for **43**.2, 10
    and online gambling **29**.12, 13
    and safety for children **104**.19
    thefts of **83**.7, 18, 32
    tracking of **82**.19-20
    and young travellers **109**.13
models of disability **91**.6, 29
moderate exercise **113**.25, 39
money
    and the cashless society **74**.9-11
    and children **74**.4, 5-6, 6-7, 12-13
    financial abuse **105**.13; **108**.7, 15
    financial planning **74**.14-39
    and lone parents **75**.37-8, 39
    students **74**.1, 17, 19-22, 28-32, 34-9
    see also banks; credit; debt; incomes; wages
monoamine oxidase inhibitors (MAOIs) **125**.32
monogamy, and marriage **106**.18-19
monophobia **84**.16, 17
mood stabilising drugs **125**.19, 25
Moonies **94**.19, 20
morbidity and coronary heart disease **113**.19
Mormons (Church of Jesus Christ of Latter-Day Saints)
    94.1, 19
morning after pill (emergency contraception) **75**.3, 13,
    15-16, 17; **126**.24
mortgages
    and first-time buyers **85**.6, 7
    and interest rates **85**.6
    and single people **85**.7
mothers
    employment patterns **107**.26; **112**.12
    full-time **124**.12

Volume numbers appear first (in bold) followed by page numbers; a change in volume number is preceded by a semi-colon.

Vol. **19** Looking at Vegetarianism
Vol. **20** Population Growth
Vol. **22** Confronting Child Abuse
Vol. **29** Gambling
Vol. **43** A Consumer Society
Vol. **60** Confronting Cancer
Vol. **69** The Media
Vol. **74** Money Matters
Vol. **75** Lone-Parent Families
Vol. **76** The Water Crisis
Vol. **77** Self-inflicted Violence
Vol. **78** Threatened Species
Vol. **79** Dealing with Homelessness
Vol. **80** The Cannabis Debate
Vol. **81** Alternative Therapies
Vol. **82** Protecting our Privacy
Vol. **83** Dealing with Crime
Vol. **84** Mental Wellbeing
Vol. **85** The Housing Crisis
Vol. **86** Smoking and your Health
Vol. **87** Genetic Modification

Vol. **88** Food and Nutrition
Vol. **89** Refugees
Vol. **90** Human and Animal Cloning
Vol. **91** Disability Issues
Vol. **92** Terrorism
Vol. **93** Binge Drinking
Vol. **94** Religions and Beliefs in Britain
Vol. **95** The Climate Crisis
Vol. **96** Preventing Sexual Diseases
Vol. **97** Energy Matters
Vol. **98** The Globalisation Issue
Vol. **99** Exploited Children
Vol. **100** Stress and Anxiety
Vol. **101** Sexuality and Discrimination
Vol. **102** The Ethics of Euthanasia
Vol. **103** Animal Rights
Vol. **104** Our Internet Society
Vol. **105** Ageing Issues
Vol. **106** Trends in Marriage
Vol. **107** Work Issues
Vol. **108** Domestic Violence

Vol. **109** Responsible Tourism
Vol. **110** Poverty
Vol. **111** The Waste Problem
Vol. **112** Women, Men and Equality
Vol. **113** Fitness and Health
Vol. **114** Drug Abuse
Vol. **115** Racial Discrimination
Vol. **116** Grief and Loss
Vol. **117** Self-Esteem and Body Image
Vol. **118** Focus on Sport
Vol. **119** Transport Trends
Vol. **120** The Human Rights Issue
Vol. **121** The Censorship Debate
Vol. **122** Bullying
Vol. **123** Young People and Health
Vol. **124** Parenting Issues
Vol. **125** Understanding Depression
Vol. **126** The Abortion Debate
Vol. **127** Eating Disorders

and poverty **110**.11, 17
    share of household tasks **124**.11
    single mothers and poverty **110**.17
    see also working mothers
motor neurone disease (MND) **90**.22
motoring costs **119**.14
motoring trends **119**.7-9
    see also cars
motorways, active traffic management **119**.37
mourning *see* grief
mouth cancer **60**.5, 15
movie trafficking, and the Internet **104**.38-9
multiculturalism
    British Muslims support for **115**.34
    London **115**.23
multinational water corporations, and the privatisation
    of water supplies **76**.22, 23, 29-30
multiple sclerosis (MS)
    and complementary medicine **81**.30-1
    and depression **125**.5
    and the medicinal use of cannabis **80**.35
multiracial families **124**.36-7
multiracialism, Britain **115**.3, 23, 24-5, 38
murder, bereavement by **116**.8
muscle strength training **113**.23
muscular endurance **113**.24
music, and raising self-esteem **117**.33
Muslims
    fears after London bombings **115**.36
    support for integration **115**.34

N

nalbuphine hydrochloride **118**.35
names for racial identity **115**.4-5
nandrolone precursors **118**.35
nappies, environmental impact **111**.13-15
narcotic analgesics **118**.38
nasal decongestants and ecstasy **114**.16
national identity
    non-white ethnic groups **115**.38
    register **120**.35
National Lottery **43**.11
    age restrictions **29**.2, 4, 27
        under 16s understanding of **29**.35-6
    and the image of gambling **29**.19
    Instants™ **29**.4, 6, 21, 35
    online **29**.12, 21
    players
        expenditure **29**.8, 9, 35
        percentage of the population **29**.3, 4, 7, 8
    and problem gamblers **29**.9, 19, 21, 26
        under 16s **29**.34-6
    and television **29**.19, 35
    and young people **29**.21, 26, 34-6
nationalist terrorism **92**.2, 7
natural cloning **90**.2
natural gas vehicles **119**.20-21
natural medicine *see* complementary medicine (CM)

natural resources **98**.21; **111**.4
    and poverty reduction **110**.25-6
naturopathy **81**.2, 19
needs, children **120**.2
neglect, and older people **105**.13
nematodes **87**.24
nervous system diseases and depression **125**.5
neuroblastoma in children **60**.9, 10
news manipulation **121**.6
newspapers
    cartoons of Mohammed **121**.10-13, 15-16
    letters pages **69**.31-2
    ownership **121**.4-5
    and press self-regulation **69**.30
    and radio **69**.21
    readership **69**.28-9
    and the tabloid press **69**.22
    the UK press **69**.24, 28-30
NGOs (non-governmental organisations), and global
    water supplies **76**.30, 31
nicotine **114**.5
    addiction **86**.2, 10
    effects of **86**.4
    gum **86**.26
    patches **86**.26
    replacement therapy **86**.3, 27, 37
    withdrawal symptoms **86**.30, 35, 36
night eating syndrome **127**.17-18
nitrogen oxide (NOx) emissions, transport **119**.15, 16
nitrous oxide, and global warming **95**.1, 4, 6, 9
no-blame policy and bullying **122**.12
no-torture agreements and deportation **120**.38
non-contributory benefits **110**.18
Non-Hodgkin's lymphoma **60**.4, 9, 10
non-means tested benefits **110**.18
non-renewable resources **111**.4
non-traditional families **124**.20-21
non-traditional jobs for women **112**.21, 25-7
NRMs (New Religious Movements) **94**.19-25
    and anti-cult movements **94**.21
    and anti-discrimination legislation **94**.35, 36
    changes in **94**.19-20
    characteristics associated with **94**.19
    cults and mind control **94**.22-3
    cults recruiting from universities **94**.24-5
    dangers associated with **94**.20-1
    defining **94**.19
    diversity among **94**.19
    joining **94**.20-2
    members in the UK **94**.21
nuclear power **95**.5, 34; **97**.3-4, 19-23
    building new power stations **97**.21-2
    and clean-up of nuclear weapons material **97**.23
    and climate change **97**.19-20, 21, 22
    costs of **97**.6
    debate over **97**.7
    disadvantages of **97**.2, 7, 8
    and electricity generation **97**.3-4, 22-3
    environmental issues surrounding **97**.2, 4
    and nuclear waste **97**.20, 22, 23
    and radioactive discharges **97**.20

and renewable energy **97**.6, 7, 19, 21
and terrorism **97**.20
nutritional supplements **118**.28
and anti-doping rules **118**.33

O

obesity **88**.4, 9-11; **113**.1-5, 6, 7-12, 15; **127**.32-9
and Body Mass Index (BMI) **113**.9, 11
in children *see* childhood obesity
and coronary heart disease **113**.20
defining **113**.9, 11; **127**.33
economic costs **88**.4; **127**.33-4, 37
and employment **113**.17, 18
and genetics **127**.35
and health **113**.5, 7, 10; **127**.32, 34
and life expectancy **105**.30
measurement **113**.7, 9, 11, 15
children **127**. 36, 37
risk groups **113**.9-10
statistics **113**.2, 9-10, 11-12; **127**.32, 33, 34
children **113**.3, 12
treatment strategies **113**.12
and worker productivity **113**.18
and young people **123**.31
obestatin (appetite-suppressing hormone) **127**.38-9
obsessive compulsive disorder (OCD) **84**.3, 9, 16
occupational choice, non-traditional
men **112**.23-4
women **112**.21, 25-7
oesophageal cancer **60**.4, 15, 17
offences, drug misuse **114**.31
offending and mental health problems **125**.16
offensive language, television **121**.38-9
offices, waste prevention **111**.16
offshore wind farms **97**.12, 16, 26
oil
depletion of resources **97**.8, 10
leakages **97**.3
oil production and climate change **95**.16-17

recycling **111**.24, 35
and renewable energy **97**.10
older people
in care homes **105**.15
and depression **125**.22-3
and health **105**.3, 5, 28-39
and mental health problems **125**.16
and money matters **105**.34
poverty **110**.19-20
women **112**.20
at risk of abuse **105**.13-14
statistics **105**.4-6
older workers **105**.16-27; **107**.12-13
and flexible working **105**.19-20, 27
and legislation on age discrimination **105**.18, 20, 23-4, 26
women **105**.21-2
online bullying **122**.19-26
open marriages **106**.18-19
organ donation **116**.31
organ transplants *see* therapeutic cloning
organic farms **87**.23-4, 28
organic food **88**.13-14, 18, 33, 34
organic waste **111**.4, 23
composting **111**.6, 23, 31, 33
Orthodox Churches **94**.1, 2
orthorexia nervosa **127**.19
osteopathy **81**.6-7, 23, 36
osteoporosis **19**.17, 18; **105**.3, 32
overexercise **113**.23, 27-8, 27-8
overweight people **127**.32, 33
children **119**.31
and coronary heart disease **113**.20
health of **113**.16
ownership of the media **121**.4-5

P

packaging
food **111**.11

Volume numbers appear first (in bold) followed by page numbers; a change in volume number is preceded by a semi-colon.

Vol. 19 Looking at Vegetarianism
Vol. 20 Population Growth
Vol. 22 Confronting Child Abuse
Vol. 29 Gambling
Vol. 43 A Consumer Society
Vol. 60 Confronting Cancer
Vol. 69 The Media
Vol. 74 Money Matters
Vol. 75 Lone-Parent Families
Vol. 76 The Water Crisis
Vol. 77 Self-inflicted Violence
Vol. 78 Threatened Species
Vol. 79 Dealing with Homelessness
Vol. 80 The Cannabis Debate
Vol. 81 Alternative Therapies
Vol. 82 Protecting our Privacy
Vol. 83 Dealing with Crime
Vol. 84 Mental Wellbeing
Vol. 85 The Housing Crisis
Vol. 86 Smoking and your Health
Vol. 87 Genetic Modification

Vol. 88 Food and Nutrition
Vol. 89 Refugees
Vol. 90 Human and Animal Cloning
Vol. 91 Disability Issues
Vol. 92 Terrorism
Vol. 93 Binge Drinking
Vol. 94 Religions and Beliefs in Britain
Vol. 95 The Climate Crisis
Vol. 96 Preventing Sexual Diseases
Vol. 97 Energy Matters
Vol. 98 The Globalisation Issue
Vol. 99 Exploited Children
Vol. 100 Stress and Anxiety
Vol. 101 Sexuality and Discrimination
Vol. 102 The Ethics of Euthanasia
Vol. 103 Animal Rights
Vol. 104 Our Internet Society
Vol. 105 Ageing Issues
Vol. 106 Trends in Marriage
Vol. 107 Work Issues
Vol. 108 Domestic Violence

Vol. 109 Responsible Tourism
Vol. 110 Poverty
Vol. 111 The Waste Problem
Vol. 112 Women, Men and Equality
Vol. 113 Fitness and Health
Vol. 114 Drug Abuse
Vol. 115 Racial Discrimination
Vol. 116 Grief and Loss
Vol. 117 Self-Esteem and Body Image
Vol. 118 Focus on Sport
Vol. 119 Transport Trends
Vol. 120 The Human Rights Issue
Vol. 121 The Censorship Debate
Vol. 122 Bullying
Vol. 123 Young People and Health
Vol. 124 Parenting Issues
Vol. 125 Understanding Depression
Vol. 126 The Abortion Debate
Vol. 127 Eating Disorders

waste **111**.5, 10, 22
paedophiles **22**.28-40
    characteristics of **22**.28
    and homosexuality **101**.17
    on the Internet **22**.31-2, 33
        'anti-grooming' orders **22**.38, 39
        and 'paedophile-free' chatrooms **22**.35, 38
        posing as children **22**.38, 39
    protecting children from **22**.28-9
    see also child pornography; sex offenders
Paganism **94**.2
pain and exercise **113**.28
pain relief
    and acupuncture **81**.5
    and cannabis **80**.22, 26, 37
    and euthanasia **102**.29, 31
    right to **102**.4-5
Palestinian terrorist groups
    Hamas **92**.2, 20, 21
    and suicide attacks **92**.15-16
palliative care
    and death with dignity **102**.30
    and terminal illnesses **102**.9, 12-13
pancreatic cancer **60**.4, 16, 17
panic disorder **84**.16
paper
    packaging waste **111**.11
    recycling **111**.24, 27, 31, 32, 36
parental leave **107**.21
parental responsibility **124**.4
parenting **124**.1-19
parents
    and adult children **124**.3, 14-15
    and advertisements targeting children **43**.9; **69**.12, 13
    and alcohol
        influence on young people **93**.17
        and young binge drinkers **93**.12, 14
    authoritarian **124**.8
    authoritative **124**.8
    of bullies **122**.8-9
    and child labour **99**.3
    and childminders **22**.22, 23-4
    and children as consumers **43**.6, 7
    and children's diet **113**.4, 8
    and children's gender development **112**.35
    and children's participation **120**.10
    and children's television viewing **121**.26, 27, 32
    and children's video game use **121**.32-3
    cohabiting and married **106**.21-2
    dealing with suspected child abuse **22**.21
    death of **116**.12-13
    divorcing **106**.33-8
    of drug users **114**.24
    fears over child safety **124**.13-14
    feelings of failure **124**.16-17
    homosexuality and the repeal of section 28 **101**.18
    and the Internet **69**.3
        and online learning **104**.9-10
        and online safety **104**.19, 20-1
        skills gap between parents and children **104**.4
    of lesbians and gays

    and choice **101**.15-16
        coming out to **101**.2-3, 11, 12, 13
        and emotions **101**.16-17
    and mobile phone tracking **82**.20
    and money matters
        savings **74**.7
        teaching children about **74**.1, 5-6
    non-traditional families **124**.20-21
    parenting skills **124**.2
    parenting styles **124**.8
    permissive **124**.8
    and the physical punishment of children **22**.22, 23-4, 25, 26, 27
    and pregnant teenagers **126**.28, 29
    protecting children from paedophiles **22**.28-9, 35, 36, 38
    and RE (religious education) **94**.15
    responsibilities **124**.4, 5
    and young fathers **75**.12
    same-sex partnerships and the right to parenthood **101**.9, 31
    and stress **100**.13
    and student money management **74**.19, 38
    and suicide of children **77**.36-8
    support for **120**.13; **124**.5, 6, 16-17
    of teenagers **124**.16-17
    unmarried **124**.22
    weight, and children's obesity **113**.3
    young people's respect for **83**.18
    see also birth parents; divorce; families; fathers; lone parents; mothers; working parents
Parkinson's disease
    and depression **125**.5
    and ecstasy **114**.4
part-time jobs **107**.17, 18, 19, 22
    children and teenagers with **74**.6, 8, 9
    and older people **105**.20
    and the pay gap **112**.17
    and students **74**.20, 37
participation rights, children **120**.9-11
participation in sport **118**.9
    adults **118**.1
    female **118**.18-20
    school team sports **118**.4
    young people **118**.2; **123**.2
particulates emissions **119**.15
passive euthanasia, religious views on **102**.2, 12
passive smoking **86**.3, 12-13, 17-18, 23, 24-5
    effect on children **123**.12
passports **89**.33
    and identity cards **82**.9-10, 12
passwords
    and children **104**.27
    and e-shopping **104**.6
    and pharming **104**.34
patent rights **87**.29, 32
paternity leave **107**.21
pay gap **112**.16-17, 20
pedestrians and road accidents **119**.5, 30-31
peer pressure
    and children's food choices **123**.32
    and sexual intercourse **123**.21

peer support and bullying **122**.12

penalties
    for drug smuggling **114**.35
    for littering **111**.19
    possession of drugs **114**.36

pensions **89**.23; **110**.19, 20
    increase in the number of pensioners **43**.3
    and the longevity revolution **105**.36
    pension crisis **105**.19, 25, 26
    and same-sex partnerships **101**.30, 34
    state pensions **105**.5, 19, 25
    and women **112**.20
    and young people **74**.1-2

Pentecostalism **94**.2

peptide hormones and analogues **118**.37

permafrost, and climate change **95**.15, 19, 24

permissive parenting style **124**.8

persistent poverty **110**.6, 13

pesticides **87**.7, 19, 23, 24, 25, 29; **88**.13, 32, 34, 35

petrol prices **119**.12-13, 14
    see also fuel taxes

pets, death of **116**.13-14

pharmaceutical industry
    and animal experiments **103**.9, 12-14
    and herbal medicine **81**.11

pharming **104**.33-4

phishing **104**.32-3

phobias **84**.9, 16, 17
    and young people **100**.2

physical abuse **108**.5, 19
    of children **22**.7, 9, 12, 13, 27
    effect on children **108**.19
    and older people **105**.13
    and self-harm **77**.14
    and stress **100**.1, 2

physical activity *see* exercise

physical addiction to drugs **114**.17-18

physical signs of bullying **122**.13, 30, 31

physician-assisted suicide (PAS) **102**.4, 7, 9
    arguments against **102**.23
    arguments for **102**.22-3
    defining **102**.22

    and euthanasia **102**.22
    and the law **102**.15, 21, 23
    and the medical profession **102**.20-1, 23, 27
    statistics **102**.17
    see also assisted suicide

phytochemicals **88**.5, 7, 13

pica **127**.17

pigeons, feeding on waste **111**.12-13

pill, contraceptive **123**.23
    and age of women **75**.15; **86**.9, 25
    morning-after (emergency contraception) **75**.3, 13,
        15-16, 17

plants
    and climate change **95**.3, 9, 11, 14-15
    endangered species **78**.2-3, 7
    and photosynthesis **97**.9
    in tropical rainforests **78**.11
    see also genetically modified (GM) crops

plastic bottles recycling **111**.26-7

plastic surgery *see* cosmetic surgery

plastic waste **111**.2, 12, 23
    and energy production **111**.2
    recycling 26-7, 31, 36

playing fields **118**.5-6

pneumonia **105**.2

pocket money **74**.6, 8, 9, 13, 14

police
    and asylum communities **89**.20
    and binge drinking **93**.2, 21
    and cannabis
        guidelines on policing **80**.30, 31, 34
        home cultivation of **80**.32-3
        possession **80**.5, 7, 8, 23, 24-5, 30
        powers of arrest **80**.30, 31, 34
        reclassification **80**.29-30, 34
        and under 18s **80**.7, 25, 30, 31, 34
    and child abuse **22**.5, 17
    and child protection on the Internet **104**.28-9
    and counter-terrorism **92**.33, 34, 38
        and the Muslim community **92**.28, 29
    and crime prevention **83**.32
    and drugs offences **114**.36

Volume numbers appear first (in bold) followed by page numbers; a change in volume number is preceded by a semi-colon.

Vol. **19** Looking at Vegetarianism
Vol. **20** Population Growth
Vol. **22** Confronting Child Abuse
Vol. **29** Gambling
Vol. **43** A Consumer Society
Vol. **60** Confronting Cancer
Vol. **69** The Media
Vol. **74** Money Matters
Vol. **75** Lone-Parent Families
Vol. **76** The Water Crisis
Vol. **77** Self-inflicted Violence
Vol. **78** Threatened Species
Vol. **79** Dealing with Homelessness
Vol. **80** The Cannabis Debate
Vol. **81** Alternative Therapies
Vol. **82** Protecting our Privacy
Vol. **83** Dealing with Crime
Vol. **84** Mental Wellbeing
Vol. **85** The Housing Crisis
Vol. **86** Smoking and your Health
Vol. **87** Genetic Modification

Vol. **88** Food and Nutrition
Vol. **89** Refugees
Vol. **90** Human and Animal Cloning
Vol. **91** Disability Issues
Vol. **92** Terrorism
Vol. **93** Binge Drinking
Vol. **94** Religions and Beliefs in Britain
Vol. **95** The Climate Crisis
Vol. **96** Preventing Sexual Diseases
Vol. **97** Energy Matters
Vol. **98** The Globalisation Issue
Vol. **99** Exploited Children
Vol. **100** Stress and Anxiety
Vol. **101** Sexuality and Discrimination
Vol. **102** The Ethics of Euthanasia
Vol. **103** Animal Rights
Vol. **104** Our Internet Society
Vol. **105** Ageing Issues
Vol. **106** Trends in Marriage
Vol. **107** Work Issues
Vol. **108** Domestic Violence

Vol. **109** Responsible Tourism
Vol. **110** Poverty
Vol. **111** The Waste Problem
Vol. **112** Women, Men and Equality
Vol. **113** Fitness and Health
Vol. **114** Drug Abuse
Vol. **115** Racial Discrimination
Vol. **116** Grief and Loss
Vol. **117** Self-Esteem and Body Image
Vol. **118** Focus on Sport
Vol. **119** Transport Trends
Vol. **120** The Human Rights Issue
Vol. **121** The Censorship Debate
Vol. **122** Bullying
Vol. **123** Young People and Health
Vol. **124** Parenting Issues
Vol. **125** Understanding Depression
Vol. **126** The Abortion Debate
Vol. **127** Eating Disorders

and football hooliganism **118**.8
and gun crime **83**.4
and identity cards **82**.8
and the Internet
‘anti-grooming’ orders **22**.38, 39
and ‘paedophile-free’ chatrooms **22**.35
and the law on hunting **103**.31
and online child pornography **99**.24
and racism in the police force **83**.12
and reported crime **83**.2, 6, 7
reporting abuse to **108**.10
shooting of police officers **83**.4
and suicide **77**.1, 36
and surveillance **82**.23
and violent crime **83**.3, 4
women in police force **112**.18
and yob-culture Britain **83**.6
politics
cannabis legalisation debate **80**.4-6
and competitive sport **118**.4
and free speech **121**.7
and support of media companies **121**.5
women in **112**.18, 39
pollution
from aviation **119**.16
and endangered species **78**.6
in the UK **78**.28, 29, 32
and population growth **20**.14, 23, 24
and species extinction **78**.11
and transport **119**.12, 13-14, 16, 30, 31
see also emissions, transport, air pollution water pollution
polydrug use **114**.2, 16-17
poppers
and the law **114**.32
and viagra **114**.16
population changes
gender ratios **43**.2, 3
population growth **20**.1-40; **89**.31
and AIDS **20**.3, 5, 7, 11
and endangered species **78**.1
and global warming **95**.9
and global water shortages **76**.3, 5, 8, 15
and immigration **20**.4-5, 11, 15-16, 32
and migration **85**.29, 30
and population density **20**.2
rates of **20**.1, 4, 7, 10, 20, 25, 26, 33, 36
and water consumption **76**.22, 29
population migration **98**.2
population studies (epidemology) **103**.17, 18, 19, 22
pornography
and the Internet
arrests and convictions **104**.29
and children and young people **104**.4, 18, 23, 24, 25, 26-7
R18 films **121**.25, 20
see also child pornography
possession of drugs **114**.36
post-mortem examination **116**.32
post-natal depression **84**.7, 9, 19; **125**.4, 17-18
diagnosis of **125**.17
symptoms of **125**.17

treatment for **125**.17-18
post-traumatic stress disorder (PTSD) **84**.9, 17; **108**.2; **116**.10
poverty **91**.9; **98**.5-6, 18
and affordable housing
in rural areas **85**.5
causes of **110**.22
and child labour **99**.2, 3, 4, 14-15; **120**.19
children living in **106**.3
defining and measuring **110**.1, 21, 22, 29
and elderly people **110**.19-20
eradication **87**.28-30, 36
global **110**.21-39
and global warming **95**.9, 35
and globalisation **98**.1, 13, 35-6
and health **110**.35
and HIV/AIDS **96**.24, 29
and homelessness **79**.4
incomes **98**.5, 13, 18, 32, 33
and international trade **98**.9, 14, 15, 21
and lone parents **75**.31, 32, 39
measuring **110**.1, 29
and Millennium Development Goals **110**.29-30
older people living in **105**.4-5, 25
and population growth **20**.9, 33
public opinions **110**.34
reduction **110**.23
and natural resources **110**.25-6
statistics **110**.29
targets **110**.6-7, 21, 23, 28, 29-31
of the rich **110**.22-3
rich-poor gap **98**.33-4
and segregation **115**.30, 31, 32
and the sexual exploitation of children **99**.16, 24
statistics **110**.2, 21, 23, 29
global **110**.35, 36
UK **110**.2, 7
and teenage pregnancy and parenthood **75**.1, 5, 10
in the UK **110**.1-20
and water
and development aid **76**.30-1
multinational water corporations **76**.29
supplies in developing countries **76**.6
and women **110**.11, 17-18, 19, 22
see also child poverty; inequality
poverty line **110**.1, 12, 22
power and self-esteem **117**.4, 31-2
Prader-Willi Syndrome **127**.17
pregnancy
and alcohol consumption **93**.4, 27
and cannabis **80**.15, 19
development **126**.26
and HIV **96**.16, 22, 23, 31, 38
and male depression **125**.14
men's rights **126**.15
and poverty **110**.11
and smoking **86**.4, 24, 25, 38; **88**.7
teenage **126**.30-31
unplanned, options **126**.9-10
see also abortion; teenage pregnancies
prejudice

definition **115**.4

in childhood, and low self-esteem **117**.32

and homophobic bullying **101**.3

Islamaphobia **115**.36

premature deaths from coronary heart disease **113**.19

prenuptial contracts **106**.22-4

pressure on athletes to use drugs **118**.29

prices, drugs **114**.6-7

falling **114**.9, 22

primary schools

gender gap **112**.8

pupil behaviour **120**.16

and sex education **75**.24

see also schools

prisoners

children in prison (under 18s) **83**.23

costs of prison **83**.8

families of **83**.39

long-term **83**.9

re-offending rates **83**.8, 10

rise in the prison population **83**.9-10

young people in prison (18-20 year olds) **83**.23

youth justice and custodial sentences **83**.24, 25

prisons

and children **120**.12

sentences for cannabis possession **80**.30, 34

privacy

children's right to **120**.12

and the media **69**.38-9

see also freedom of information

privacy rights **82**.1-3, 39

bodily privacy **82**.5

and communications data **82**.1-2

communications privacy **82**.5

comprehensive laws on **82**.5

defining privacy **82**.4

and human rights **82**.4-5, 18

information privacy **82**.5

models of privacy protection **82**.5

and RFID tags **82**.13-17, 35

and technologies of privacy **82**.5

viewpoints on privacy **82**.4

in the workplace **82**.25-30

private communication interception **120**.34

privatisation

impact on poverty **110**.22

and water management **76**.22-3, 32

criticisms of private companies **76**.32

multinational water corporations **76**.22, 23, 29-30

pro-life arguments **126**.21-2

pro-life movement **126**.25

pro-poor tourism **109**.27, 38

prosecutions for littering **111**.9

prostate cancer **60**.3, 4, 6, 24-5; **105**.10

prostitution and child sex tourism **109**.35

protection of children

from abuse **120**.14-15

refugees **120**.22

protectionism **98**.9, 10-11, 24

protectiveness, parental **124**.13-14

proteins **88**.6, 8

excessive **19**.15-16

and vegans **19**.13, 16

and vegetarians **19**.9

Protestant traditions and beliefs **94**.1, 2

psilocin **114**.35

psilocybin **114**.35

psychiatrists, and mental illness **84**.25-6

psychological abuse and older people **105**.13

psychological addiction to drugs **114**.18

psychological bullying **122**.10

psychological conditions and eating disorders **127**.9-10

psychological distress caused by obesity **113**.7

psychological health requirements **117**.8

psychological treatment for self-harm **77**.25

psychologists, and young people and stress **100**.2

psychosis **84**.8-9

cannabis link to **80**.17, 19; **38**

psychosurgery **125**.26

psychotherapy

and mental illness **84**.10

as a treatment for depression **125**.7, 26, 33

and young people and stress **100**.2

puberty **127**.22

Volume numbers appear first (in bold) followed by page numbers; a change in volume number is preceded by a semi-colon.

Vol. **19** Looking at Vegetarianism

Vol. **20** Population Growth

Vol. **22** Confronting Child Abuse

Vol. **29** Gambling

Vol. **43** A Consumer Society

Vol. **60** Confronting Cancer

Vol. **69** The Media

Vol. **74** Money Matters

Vol. **75** Lone-Parent Families

Vol. **76** The Water Crisis

Vol. **77** Self-inflicted Violence

Vol. **78** Threatened Species

Vol. **79** Dealing with Homelessness

Vol. **80** The Cannabis Debate

Vol. **81** Alternative Therapies

Vol. **82** Protecting our Privacy

Vol. **83** Dealing with Crime

Vol. **84** Mental Wellbeing

Vol. **85** The Housing Crisis

Vol. **86** Smoking and your Health

Vol. **87** Genetic Modification

Vol. **88** Food and Nutrition

Vol. **89** Refugees

Vol. **90** Human and Animal Cloning

Vol. **91** Disability Issues

Vol. **92** Terrorism

Vol. **93** Binge Drinking

Vol. **94** Religions and Beliefs in Britain

Vol. **95** The Climate Crisis

Vol. **96** Preventing Sexual Diseases

Vol. **97** Energy Matters

Vol. **98** The Globalisation Issue

Vol. **99** Exploited Children

Vol. **100** Stress and Anxiety

Vol. **101** Sexuality and Discrimination

Vol. **102** The Ethics of Euthanasia

Vol. **103** Animal Rights

Vol. **104** Our Internet Society

Vol. **105** Ageing Issues

Vol. **106** Trends in Marriage

Vol. **107** Work Issues

Vol. **108** Domestic Violence

Vol. **109** Responsible Tourism

Vol. **110** Poverty

Vol. **111** The Waste Problem

Vol. **112** Women, Men and Equality

Vol. **113** Fitness and Health

Vol. **114** Drug Abuse

Vol. **115** Racial Discrimination

Vol. **116** Grief and Loss

Vol. **117** Self-Esteem and Body Image

Vol. **118** Focus on Sport

Vol. **119** Transport Trends

Vol. **120** The Human Rights Issue

Vol. **121** The Censorship Debate

Vol. **122** Bullying

Vol. **123** Young People and Health

Vol. **124** Parenting Issues

Vol. **125** Understanding Depression

Vol. **126** The Abortion Debate

Vol. **127** Eating Disorders

and eating disorders **127**.2, 22-4
public attitudes
to advertising **69**.14-15
to childminders and disciplining children **22**.23-4
to consumer rights **43**.14, 15-16
to film classification **121**.24
to GM foods **87**.3-4, 5-7, 16
to healthy eating campaigns **113**.13
to homeless people **79**.4, 32
to Internet use **104**.15
to marriage and cohabitation **106**.4-6
to refugees **89**.17
to world poverty **110**.34
public grief **116**.17-18
public policing, littering **111**.8
public safety and censorship **121**.13
public transport **119**.1, 12, 25
encouraging use of **119**.39

Q

Quakers (Religious Society of Friends) **94**.2
qualifications **89**.34-5; **107**.1, 34
gender differences **112**.1, 8
quality of life, and euthanasia **102**.2, 29, 30
quitting smoking **86**.3, 6, 9, 14, 27-30, 33-7
Qu'ran (Koran) **94**.2, 10
and terrorism **92**.26, 29, 37

R

R18 film classification **121**.25, 30
race
definition **115**.4
as grounds for discrimination **115**.7
names for **115**.4-5
race hate trials **121**.15
racial background, UK population **115**.3, 24-5
racial discrimination **115**.4, 7-8
and academic freedom **121**.8, 9
in employment **115**.13
see also racism
racial equality in football **118**.15-16
racial harassment
defining **115**.8
of refugees **89**.19, 20
racial integration **107**.12; **115**.6, 28-9
Asians **115**.37
in education **115**.29, 33
racial segregation **115**.28-32
racially motivated crime **115**.9-10
racism **115**.1-2, 4
challenging **115**.2
and children **115**.9
defining **115**.4
and education **115**.19-20
effects of **115**.1

in football **118**.14
and Islamophobia **94**.34-5; **115**.36
laws **115**.2, 7-8, 11-12, 26
reasons for **115**.1-2
in schools **115**.9, 19-20
in the workplace **115**.11-14
see also discrimination; employment and racism; ethnic
minorities; racial discrimination
racist bullying **115**.2; **122**.4-5
rainfall
and climate change **95**.2-3, 7, 14, 16
and water distribution in the UK **76**.1-2
rainforests *see* forestry
rape
marital rape **108**.6
statutory **101**.27
and women's economic autonomy **112**.38
see also sexual violence
Rastafarians **94**.2
RE (religious education) **94**.9-10, 15, 31, 37
reactive depression **84**.7; **125**.4
recruitment of employees, discrimination **115**.13
recycling **111**.4, 15, 17, 22-37
aluminium **111**.11, 23-4, 26
cans **111**.11, 23, 26
collections **111**.3, 29
glass **111**.11, 23, 27, 28, 31, 36
household waste **111**.6
incentives **111**.34, 37
oil **111**.24, 35
organic waste *see* composting waste
paper **111**.24, 27, 31, 32, 36
plastic **111**.26-7, 31, 36
targets **111**.37
reduce, reuse, recycle **111**.1, 3
reducing waste **111**.4, 17
businesses **111**.18
reflexology **81**.3, 15-17, 23, 36
and stress-related illnesses **81**.16
training as a reflexologist **81**.16-17
refugees **120**.31
children **120**.21-2
and climate change **95**.12, 15, 17
and population growth **20**.11
see also asylum seekers
refuges **108**.21, 32-3, 34-5, 37
regulation
of children's viewing **121**.26-7
film **121**.22-5, 29-30
television **121**.36-7
video **121**.26, 31
video games **121**.32-3
relationship support **106**.29-30
relative poverty **110**.21, 22-3
relaxation
as help for depression **125**.39
coping with stress **100**.29-30, 31-2, 34, 36-7
and self-esteem **117**.35, 37
religion
and abortion **126**.1-3, 6
and the Census (2001) **94**.3, 5-6, 28

and children's rights **120**.2
and depression in older people **105**.39
and euthanasia
    assisted suicide **102**.17
    and the killing of disabled babies **102**.26
    religious views on **102**.2, 8-9, 12-14, 17, 18
and food rules **94**.10
funeral traditions **116**.33-5
and GM crops **87**.3
homosexuality and the Church **101**.6, 15, 18, 29
and life expectancy **105**.29
myths about **94**.8-9
and terrorism **92**.2-3, 6, 15-16; **94**.10
and humanism **94**.39
legislation **94**.27-8, 29, 32, 35-6
and religious tolerance **94**.26
religious discrimination **115**.26
religious education *see* RE (religious education)
religious festivals **94**.3-4
    legislation on time off work for **94**.35-6
religious groups segregation **115**.32
religious identity **115**.5, 26
religious tolerance **94**.26-39
    definitions of **94**.26-7
    and faith-based schools **94**.30-1
    and humanism **94**.38-9
    and Islamophobia **94**.33
religiously motivated crime **115**.27
renewable energy **95**.34, 36; **97**.6-18, 26
    advantages of **97**.9
    attitudes to **97**.5
    bioenergy **97**.5, 6, 9, 11, 18
    case for **97**.1-2, 6-7
    costs of **97**.19, 38
    defining **97**.8-9
    electricity from **97**.4, 11, 37-8
    future of **97**.8-9
    hydroelectric power **97**.4, 5, 6, 12, 14, 38
    and nuclear power **97**.6, 7, 19, 21
    sources of **97**.4
    types of **97**.9
    in the UK **97**.13-14, 26, 39

see also energy efficiency; solar energy; wind energy
reproductive rights **20**.27-8, 35-8
reproductive system, effects of eating disorders **127**.5
research cloning **90**.3, 5, 6
responsible tourism **109**.18-39
    ecotourism **109**.19-20, 38-9
        definitions **109**.27
        glossary **109**.23-5
    and heritage sites **109**.20-2
    information on sustainable tourism **109**.28-9
    and working conditions in the tourist industry **109**.30, 31
    see also ecotourism
restaurant smoking policies **86**.17, 19, 20-3
retail industry **98**.15-16; **107**.5
retinoblastomas, and childhood cancer **60**.9, 11
retirement
    age of **105**.20, 27, 36; **107**.13
    attitudes to **105**.24
    early **105**.27
    and flexible working **105**.19-20
    and male depression **125**.15
    and the pension crisis **105**.19, 25
reusing waste **111**.4, 17
RFID (Radio Frequency Identification) tags **82**.13-17, 35
    companies making or using **82**.13, 15-16, 35
    and crime **82**.17
    and data protection **82**.16
    defining **82**.13, 15
    disabling **82**.14
    identifying **82**.13-14
    media coverage of **82**.15
    possible consumer benefits of **82**.16-17
    and surveillance **82**.16
rich-poor gap **98**.33-4
    global **110**.35
    UK **110**.13, 14, 16; **115**.32
rights
    in abortion
        of the foetus **126**.21-2, 27
        of men **126**.15
        of women **126**.21
    children's *see* children's rights

Volume numbers appear first (in bold) followed by page numbers; a change in volume number is preceded by a semi-colon.

Vol. **19** Looking at Vegetarianism
Vol. **20** Population Growth
Vol. **22** Confronting Child Abuse
Vol. **29** Gambling
Vol. **43** A Consumer Society
Vol. **60** Confronting Cancer
Vol. **69** The Media
Vol. **74** Money Matters
Vol. **75** Lone-Parent Families
Vol. **76** The Water Crisis
Vol. **77** Self-inflicted Violence
Vol. **78** Threatened Species
Vol. **79** Dealing with Homelessness
Vol. **80** The Cannabis Debate
Vol. **81** Alternative Therapies
Vol. **82** Protecting our Privacy
Vol. **83** Dealing with Crime
Vol. **84** Mental Wellbeing
Vol. **85** The Housing Crisis
Vol. **86** Smoking and your Health
Vol. **87** Genetic Modification

Vol. **88** Food and Nutrition
Vol. **89** Refugees
Vol. **90** Human and Animal Cloning
Vol. **91** Disability Issues
Vol. **92** Terrorism
Vol. **93** Binge Drinking
Vol. **94** Religions and Beliefs in Britain
Vol. **95** The Climate Crisis
Vol. **96** Preventing Sexual Diseases
Vol. **97** Energy Matters
Vol. **98** The Globalisation Issue
Vol. **99** Exploited Children
Vol. **100** Stress and Anxiety
Vol. **101** Sexuality and Discrimination
Vol. **102** The Ethics of Euthanasia
Vol. **103** Animal Rights
Vol. **104** Our Internet Society
Vol. **105** Ageing Issues
Vol. **106** Trends in Marriage
Vol. **107** Work Issues
Vol. **108** Domestic Violence

Vol. **109** Responsible Tourism
Vol. **110** Poverty
Vol. **111** The Waste Problem
Vol. **112** Women, Men and Equality
Vol. **113** Fitness and Health
Vol. **114** Drug Abuse
Vol. **115** Racial Discrimination
Vol. **116** Grief and Loss
Vol. **117** Self-Esteem and Body Image
Vol. **118** Focus on Sport
Vol. **119** Transport Trends
Vol. **120** The Human Rights Issue
Vol. **121** The Censorship Debate
Vol. **122** Bullying
Vol. **123** Young People and Health
Vol. **124** Parenting Issues
Vol. **125** Understanding Depression
Vol. **126** The Abortion Debate
Vol. **127** Eating Disorders

same-sex partnerships and the law 101.30-2
    to protest 121.14
    about offensive material 121.13
    young people 120.1-22
    see also human rights
rivers
    and climate change 95.21-2
    drying up of 76.2, 35
    pollution 76.4
      and freshwater supplies 76.15
    and species extinction 78.10
road accidents 119.4, 5, 28, 30-31
    and alcohol consumption 93.7, 8, 18
    and cannabis 80.16, 17
    and children 119.5, 28, 30-31
    deaths 119.4, 5, 28, 30
    and speed 119.5, 30-31
road charging 119.35, 36
    congestion charging 119.12, 34-5, 38
road safety 119.4
road traffic 119.1
    increase 119.11, 13, 29
    injuries, children 119.5, 28, 30-31
    see also cars
robberies
    and gun crime 83.4
    mobile phone thefts 83.7, 18, 32
    rates of 83.3
rough sleepers
    backgrounds of 79.10, 18
    health problems of 79.15
    and homelessness 79.20
    missing persons 79.14
    numbers of 79.1, 2, 5, 7, 8, 19
    young people 79.22, 23
    see also homelessness
rural areas, poverty in 110.25

S

safe sex 101.1, 17, 20
safety
    and alcohol 123.17
    and cycling 119.28
    in exercise 113.28
    parents' fears 124.13-14
    transport 119.1
    and walking to school 119.26
    at work 107.31
safety and the Internet
    boundaries and regulation 104.18
    chat and instant messaging 104.35
    children and young people 104.17-29
    computer and Internet addiction 104.36-7
    filtering software 104.19, 22, 23, 31
salmonella 88.28
salt intake 88.2, 7, 10, 16, 23, 26
    teenagers 123.7
sanctity of life argument, and euthanasia 102.2

sanitation
    in developing countries 76.7, 8, 12, 17, 21
    and the right to water 76.24
saturated fats 88.2, 22-3
savings
    attitudes to 74.5
      children 74.6-7
    and child poverty 110.13
    lack of 110.16
    and parents 74.7
    savings accounts
      for children 74.13
      and young people 74.19, 24
    and teenagers 74.8-9
    and young people 74.15
scabies 96.7
schizophrenia 84.8, 13-15; 108.2
    and alcohol 84.14
    and assisted suicide 102.6
    and cannabis 80.7, 10, 12, 14, 17, 19-20, 22, 26
    and childhood disorders 84.29
    and diet 84.14-15
    and drug abuse 84.14
    and smoking 84.14
    and suicide 77.3, 18
    symptoms 84.2-3, 4, 9
school bullying 122.1-7; 11-12
    anti-bullying policies 122.11, 18, 25
    and film violence 121.28
    girls and young women 122.10, 14, 15-16
    homophobic bullying 122.3
    no-blame policy 122.6-7
    peer support 122.12
    racist bullying 122.4-5
    and self-harm 77.6, 7, 9
school uniform and gender equality 112.10-11
schools
    abuse prevention programmes 108.24-6
    alcohol education in 93.11, 16, 35
    behaviour problems 120.16
    and children in developing countries 76.13-14
    computers in 104.11
    drug tests 114.26
    drug use 83.12
    and emergency contraception 75.17
    and ethnic minority children 115.18, 19-21
    faith-based 94.12-14, 28, 30-1, 38
    gender equality 112.9-11
    and integration 115.29, 33
    and the Internet 104.3
    journeys to 119.25, 26-7, 29-30
    and litter 111.8-9
    and mental health
      education in 84.30, 31
      positive steps to 84.27
    and online learning 104.9-10
    promoting physical activity 113.6
    and racism 115.9, 19-20
    RE (religious education) 94.9-10, 15, 31, 37
    and religious diversity 94.39
    self-harm in 77.30-1

and sexuality
    and equality for gays and lesbians **101**.21-2
    homophobic bullying **101**.3, 18, 19, 20, 21-2, 38-9
    and the repeal of section 28 **101**.18, 21, 22, 39
sports **118**.3, 4
and suicide prevention **77**.3, 33
teaching about money matters **74**.1, 6, 12, 32-3
truancy and offending **83**.14
young people's attitudes to **123**.2-3
scientific research, and animal experiments **103**.3
Scientology **94**.2-3, 17-18, 19
screen violence, influence on children **121**.28, 33, 34, 35
sea level rises **95**.1, 6, 7, 9, 11-14, 16, 25-6
Seasonal Affective Disorder (SAD) **84**.7, 17, 19; **125**.4, 18, 37-8
seasonal labour **89**.22-3
secondary schools
    gender differences **112**.1, 8
    see also schools
secularism
    and RE (religious education) **94**.9-10
    and religious discrimination legislation **94**.37-8
segregation **115**.28-32
segregation indices **115**.31-2
Selective Serotonin Re-uptake Inhibitors (SSRIs) **123**.28; **125**.8, 10, 32
self-censorship, broadcasters **121**.36-7
self-criticism **117**.6, 34
self-employment **107**.2
self-esteem **117**.1-9; **127**.24
    contributory factors **117**.4, 31-3
    definition **117**.1, 31
    and eating disorders **127**.2
    and green activities **117**.38-9
    healthy **117**.30
    high **117**.5, 31
        and criminality **117**.7
    improving **117**.1-2, 6, 33-9
    low, and bullying **122**.8
self-harm **77**.6-14, 24-31; **123**.9, 36-9
    age of self-harmers **77**.6
    defining **77**.12

and eating disorders **127**.10
and girls in prison **83**.27, 28-9
and homophobia **101**.20, 22
and men **77**.14
methods of **77**.8, 24
myths about **77**.10, 11, 12-13, 26
prevention
    changing A & E staff attitudes **77**.26
    help by friends and family **77**.28-9
    help by parents and teachers **77**.25
    helping yourself **77**.10, 27-8; **123**.37
    specialist help for **77**.25
    and young people **77**.24-5, 27-9
reasons for **77**.6-7, 9, 12, 24, 27, 30; **123**.37
in schools **77**.30-1
sources of help **123**.36-7
statistics **77**.9, 10; **84**.1
and students **77**.22
and suicide **77**.8, 9, 11, 12, 21; **123**.36
and women **77**.12-14
self-image *see* body image
separation
    effect on children **124**.33-4
    and male depression **125**.14
    and the process of divorce **106**.28
    see also divorce
separation from parents, children's rights **120**.11
September 11 2001 terrorist attacks **92**.8, 9, 11, 13, 14, 16, 22
    and counter-terrorism
        in the European Union **92**.19, 21
        in the UK **92**.30, 31-2, 33-4, 35
    and Islamophobia **92**.36
serotonin and eating disorders **127**.6-7
services
    and child labour **99**.2, 4
    consumer rights when buying a service **43**.18
    and globalisation **98**.10, 23
sex discrimination in employment **112**.13-14, 20
    see also glass ceiling, pay gap
sex education **75**.2, 20, 21-2; **123**.20
    and attitudes and beliefs **75**.18, 19, 21

Volume numbers appear first (in bold) followed by page numbers; a change in volume number is preceded by a semi-colon.

Vol. **19** Looking at Vegetarianism
Vol. **20** Population Growth
Vol. **22** Confronting Child Abuse
Vol. **29** Gambling
Vol. **43** A Consumer Society
Vol. **60** Confronting Cancer
Vol. **69** The Media
Vol. **74** Money Matters
Vol. **75** Lone-Parent Families
Vol. **76** The Water Crisis
Vol. **77** Self-inflicted Violence
Vol. **78** Threatened Species
Vol. **79** Dealing with Homelessness
Vol. **80** The Cannabis Debate
Vol. **81** Alternative Therapies
Vol. **82** Protecting our Privacy
Vol. **83** Dealing with Crime
Vol. **84** Mental Wellbeing
Vol. **85** The Housing Crisis
Vol. **86** Smoking and your Health
Vol. **87** Genetic Modification

Vol. **88** Food and Nutrition
Vol. **89** Refugees
Vol. **90** Human and Animal Cloning
Vol. **91** Disability Issues
Vol. **92** Terrorism
Vol. **93** Binge Drinking
Vol. **94** Religions and Beliefs in Britain
Vol. **95** The Climate Crisis
Vol. **96** Preventing Sexual Diseases
Vol. **97** Energy Matters
Vol. **98** The Globalisation Issue
Vol. **99** Exploited Children
Vol. **100** Stress and Anxiety
Vol. **101** Sexuality and Discrimination
Vol. **102** The Ethics of Euthanasia
Vol. **103** Animal Rights
Vol. **104** Our Internet Society
Vol. **105** Ageing Issues
Vol. **106** Trends in Marriage
Vol. **107** Work Issues
Vol. **108** Domestic Violence

Vol. **109** Responsible Tourism
Vol. **110** Poverty
Vol. **111** The Waste Problem
Vol. **112** Women, Men and Equality
Vol. **113** Fitness and Health
Vol. **114** Drug Abuse
Vol. **115** Racial Discrimination
Vol. **116** Grief and Loss
Vol. **117** Self-Esteem and Body Image
Vol. **118** Focus on Sport
Vol. **119** Transport Trends
Vol. **120** The Human Rights Issue
Vol. **121** The Censorship Debate
Vol. **122** Bullying
Vol. **123** Young People and Health
Vol. **124** Parenting Issues
Vol. **125** Understanding Depression
Vol. **126** The Abortion Debate
Vol. **127** Eating Disorders

and teenage pregnancy **75**.2-3, 13, 14, 20-2, 23
and underage sex **123**.21
sex offenders
and the child protection system **22**.30-1
treatment of **22**.5-6
sex segregation in training and work **112**.21-2
sex tourism **109**.5, 32, 35-6
sexual abuse **22**.1, 4, 14, 16, 18-19; **108**.5-6, 19, 29
characteristics of abusers **22**.16, 18
and child domestic workers **99**.8, 9
child protection registers **22**.11, 12
defining **101**.27
and self-harm **77**.10, 14; **123**.37
and siblings **22**.10, 15-16
signs and symptoms of **22**.6, 7
statistics **22**.2, 3, 10
and stress **100**.1, 2
young people **22**.13-14
and young runaways **79**.25
sexual behaviour
and abstinence education **75**.18, 26-7
and early sexual relationships **75**.17-19; **123**.21
and HIV **96**.12, 14, 16, 17
and male depression **125**.14
and sexually transmitted infections **75**.16, 17-18; **96**.9, 12
teenagers **123**.19-21
underage sex **75**.14, 17-18, 27; **123**.21
sexual exploitation of children **99**.1, 4, 16-18, 20-8
case studies **99**.21-2
harmful effects of **99**.16, 20
and poverty **99**.16, 24
and sex tourism **99**.17, 20, 23, 25-6
teenagers **99**.20-2
and trafficking **99**.3, 16, 17, 18, 20, 21, 24, 28
see also child pornography; child prostitution
sexual relationships, changing attitudes to **106**.20
sexuality
age of consent **101**.3, 27, 29
and boys' culture **112**.34
exploring **101**.1, 4
labels and stereotypes **101**.1
and the law **101**.1
sexually transmitted infections (STIs) **20**.27-8, 33-5, 39-40; **96**.1-13; **101**.3, 4; **123**.5, 24-6
and abstinence education **75**.26
avoiding **96**.1-2
bacterial **96**.3, 10, 12
chlamydia **96**.2-3, 4, 5, 8, 10, 12; **123**.26
genital herpes **96**.3, 4, 6, 10, 12
genital warts **96**.2-3, 4, 5-6, 12-13
gonorrhoea **96**.2, 3, 4, 5, 8, 10, 12
and HIV **96**.10, 12, 25
increase in **96**.4
knowledge of **75**.15-16
pubic lice **96**.7
and sex education **75**.22
and sexual behaviour **96**.9, 12
symptoms of **96**.1, 5, 6, 7
syphilis **96**.3, 4, 6, 8, 10, 12
and teenage sex **75**.17-18

testing for **96**.1, 2, 3, 5, 6, 7, 10
treatment of **96**.1, 5, 6, 7, 10
trichomonas vaginalis **96**.6-7
types of **96**.2
in the UK **96**.2-3, 4
viral **96**.12-13
and young people **96**.3, 4, 8-9; **123**.3
see also Genito-Urinary Medicine (GUM) clinics
shantytowns **20**.17-18, 20
shopping
and budgeting **74**.23
and children **43**.6-8
and energy efficiency **97**.31-2
expenditure on luxuries **43**.1, 3
from home **82**.36-7
Internet **43**.23-4, 38-9, 40; **104**.5-8
and money management **74**.17
and waste reduction **111**.16
sickness absence **107**.6-8
Sikhs **94**.6
and abortion and contraception **126**.2
beliefs **94**.3
and the Census (2001) **94**.3, 5, 28
festivals **94**.4
food rules **94**.10
funerals **116**.34
Golden Rule **94**.8
and 'honour killings' **94**.30
and RE (religious education) **94**.9
simple carbohydrates **88**.2
single homelessness **79**.5-7
case studies **79**.6-7, 16-17
and concealed households **79**.5, 7, 19
costs of **79**.5-6
legal entitlements **79**.8
and mental health problems **79**.15, 16-17
statistics **79**.5, 7, 19
single parents see lone parents
single people
and the cost of living **106**.13
growth in numbers **43**.2
and the housing market **85**.7, 23-4
lesbian, gay and bisexual **101**.9
living alone **85**.2
men **106**.3, 12, 20
women **106**.3, 20
single-sex teaching **112**.4-6
SIV (self-inflicted violence) see self-harm
skills shortages **107**.31-3
skin cancer (melanoma) **60**.5, 18, 19-21
slavery **120**.29, 30-31
and child labour **99**.1; **120**.18-19
sleep
and Internet addiction **104**.37
and life expectancy **105**.29
and stress **100**.19, 27, 29
smacking children **22**.22, 23-4, 26
smart chip cards **43**.34-5
smoking **114**.5, 29
adult smokers **86**.1, 2, 6, 14
advertising cigarettes **86**.5, 8, 26

age groups of smokers **86**.1
bans **86**.3, 13, 19-23, 38
benefits of smoking **86**.11
and cancer **60**.1, 2, 3, 14, 15-17, 27
and childminders **22**.22, 23
and children **86**.1, 8, 14-15, 24-5, 26; **123**.11-13
   starting smoking **123**.11, 13
and coronary heart disease **113**.19-20
costs of **86**.7, 25, 33
deaths from **86**.2, 9, 10, 14, 16, 17
decline in **86**.1, 2-3
health risks **86**.2, 3, 5, 6, 9-11, 13, 14-16, 24-5, 31
and life expectancy **86**.31; **105**.2, 9, 30
and litter **111**.9
in public places **86**.3, 13, 18, 19-23
and schizophrenia **84**.14
and self-harm **77**.6, 13, 26
sleeper effect **123**.13
statistics **86**.1-3, 14
stopping **86**.3, 6, 9, 14, 27-30, 33-7
and stress **100**.19, 27, 31, 34, 35, 37
and teenagers **86**.1, 2, 5-7
withdrawal symptoms **86**.30, 35, 36
women smokers **86**.1, 2, 5, 9, 14, 24, 25, 38
in the workplace **86**.17, 18, 19, 23, 25
young people **123**.2, 8, 9, 11-13
   and the law **123**.12
   prevention **123**.12, 13
social exclusion **110**.8-9
and children in prison **83**.23
and crime **83**.8
   and young people **83**.18
and crime prevention **83**.33
social inequality **110**.14
and coronary heart disease **113**.19
social justice, and climate change **95**.16, 17
social life and self-esteem **117**.36
social model of disability **91**.6, 29
social phobia **84**.16
social responsibility **98**.6, 26, 29, 37-8
social workers
and stress in young people **100**.2

and workplace stress **100**.12
socio-economic groups
and childhood obesity **113**.3
and non-traditional families **124**.21
soft segregation **115**.28
soil management **87**.35; **88**.14
solar energy **95**.34; **97**.2, 4, 6, 8-9, 10, 21
costs of **97**.14
and energy efficiency **97**.31
market for **97**.14
PV (Photovoltaics) **97**.8, 9, 12, 13, 38
in the UK **97**.10, 13, 14, 26
solar radiation **95**.1, 2, 7, 8, 15
solid fuels, as a source of energy **97**.4
solvent abuse **80**.11; **114**.21, 27-8
solvents and the law **114**.32
somatic cells, and ageing **105**.1
somatic-cell nuclear transfer (SCNT) **90**.2, 3, 6, 11, 17
soya **87**.4, 5, 9, 12, 13, 29, 31
spam **82**.31-3, 36-7; **104**.30-1
spambots (spiders) **104**.30, 31
speed (drug)
and depressants **114**.17
and ecstasy **114**.16
speed cameras **119**.4, 17, 18
speed limits
and active traffic management **119**.37-8
raising **119**.4
speeding **119**.3, 4, 8
and pedestrian injuries **119**.5, 30-31
spin, government **121**.17-18
sport
and drugs **118**.23-39
and inclusion **118**.12-22
participation *see* participation in sport
safety **113**.28
trends **118**.1-11
sporting animals, cloning **90**.30
sports facilities **118**.5-6
sports and gender equality **112**.11
spot weight reduction **113**.27
Staphylococcus aureus **88**.29

Volume numbers appear first (in bold) followed by page numbers; a change in volume number is preceded by a semi-colon.

Vol. **19** Looking at Vegetarianism
Vol. **20** Population Growth
Vol. **22** Confronting Child Abuse
Vol. **29** Gambling
Vol. **43** A Consumer Society
Vol. **60** Confronting Cancer
Vol. **69** The Media
Vol. **74** Money Matters
Vol. **75** Lone-Parent Families
Vol. **76** The Water Crisis
Vol. **77** Self-inflicted Violence
Vol. **78** Threatened Species
Vol. **79** Dealing with Homelessness
Vol. **80** The Cannabis Debate
Vol. **81** Alternative Therapies
Vol. **82** Protecting our Privacy
Vol. **83** Dealing with Crime
Vol. **84** Mental Wellbeing
Vol. **85** The Housing Crisis
Vol. **86** Smoking and your Health
Vol. **87** Genetic Modification

Vol. **88** Food and Nutrition
Vol. **89** Refugees
Vol. **90** Human and Animal Cloning
Vol. **91** Disability Issues
Vol. **92** Terrorism
Vol. **93** Binge Drinking
Vol. **94** Religions and Beliefs in Britain
Vol. **95** The Climate Crisis
Vol. **96** Preventing Sexual Diseases
Vol. **97** Energy Matters
Vol. **98** The Globalisation Issue
Vol. **99** Exploited Children
Vol. **100** Stress and Anxiety
Vol. **101** Sexuality and Discrimination
Vol. **102** The Ethics of Euthanasia
Vol. **103** Animal Rights
Vol. **104** Our Internet Society
Vol. **105** Ageing Issues
Vol. **106** Trends in Marriage
Vol. **107** Work Issues
Vol. **108** Domestic Violence

Vol. **109** Responsible Tourism
Vol. **110** Poverty
Vol. **111** The Waste Problem
Vol. **112** Women, Men and Equality
Vol. **113** Fitness and Health
Vol. **114** Drug Abuse
Vol. **115** Racial Discrimination
Vol. **116** Grief and Loss
Vol. **117** Self-Esteem and Body Image
Vol. **118** Focus on Sport
Vol. **119** Transport Trends
Vol. **120** The Human Rights Issue
Vol. **121** The Censorship Debate
Vol. **122** Bullying
Vol. **123** Young People and Health
Vol. **124** Parenting Issues
Vol. **125** Understanding Depression
Vol. **126** The Abortion Debate
Vol. **127** Eating Disorders

starchy foods **87**.20, 38; **88**.5-6, 12
state benefits **110**.18
    after bereavement **116**.30
    and child poverty **110**.4, 6, 7
    for asylum seekers **89**.12, 13, 14, 19, 30, 38
    Child Tax Credit **74**.7; **110**.6, 7
    costs of incapacity benefit **100**.23
    housing benefit **79**.9, 12
    jobseekers' allowance **100**.23
    and lone parents **75**.31
        disabled person's tax credit (DTC) **75**.38
    and older people **105**.5; **110**.19
    and students **74**.39
    and teenage mothers **75**.22
    Working Families Tax Credit **74**.7
    see also disability benefits; housing benefit
state pension **110**.19, 20
state-sponsored terrorism **92**.3, 7-8, 11
statutory rape **101**.27
steel cans recycling **111**.12, 23, 26
stem cell research **90**.3, 5, 13, 14, 15, 20-1, 22
stepfamilies **124**.23-8, 39
    benefits **124**.25
    children's worries **124**.23, 26
    parents' worries **124**.27-8
    statistics **106**.3-4; **124**.23, 24, 25
    step-parenting **124**.39
    and suicide of children **77**.38
stereotypes, gender stereotypes **108**.26
steroids *see* anabolic agents/steroids
stimulants **114**.1-2, 5, 29; **118**.36-7
stomach cancer **60**.4, 16, 17
stopping smoking **86**.3, 6, 9, 14, 27-30, 33-7
storms, and climate change **95**.2, 5, 9, 11, 15, 25
street children **99**.1, 18-19
strength training **113**.23, 27
stress **86**.11, 35; **107**.8, 18
    and anxiety **100**.2, 21
    coping with **100**.27-39
    defining **100**.1, 5, 33
    and eating disorders **127**.16
    factors determining degree of **100**.14-15
    'fight or flight' response to **100**.1, 14-15, 25, 28
    harmful effects of **100**.28, 38
    and life expectancy **105**.10, 30
    and lifestyle **100**.19, 31-2
    men **112**.30
    positive and negative **100**.14
    and self-injury **77**.27
    signs and symptoms of **100**.1, 2, 5, 12, 28-9, 33, 35
    statistics on **100**.13, 19
    and workplace bullying **122**.30, 37
stress management **100**.32, 36
strokes **105**.3
    and depression **125**.5
    and diet **19**.18
structural adjustment **98**.3, 5, 7
students **91**.35; **107**.33, 35-6
    graduate recruitment **91**.19-20
    health issues **123**.4-5
    and mental illness **84**.32-3

    and money matters **74**.1, 17, 19-22, 28-32, 34-9
        bank accounts **74**.1, 2, 17, 21-2, 29, 32
        budgeting **74**.2, 28, 30, 32
        bursaries **74**.32, 37
        costs of a university education **74**.38
        credit cards **74**.3, 30, 32, 36, 37
        disabled students **74**.39
        graduate starting salaries **74**.31
        grants **74**.39
        hardship funds **74**.37
        living and study costs **74**.28, 30
        overdrafts **74**.1, 21-2, 37
        and paid employment **74**.20, 29, 37
        and parents **74**.19, 38
        and state benefits **74**.39
        tuition fees **74**.19, 20, 31, 37, 39
        university access funds **74**.39
    opinions on abortion for disability **126**.35
    and suicide prevention **77**.15-16, 22-3
subsidies **87**.31; **98**.9, 10-11, 17, 31
substance abuse **114**.17
    and homelessness **79**.2
    and young runaways **79**.29
    young people **123**.17
    see also alcohol; drugs
suction termination (abortion) **126**.14
sugar beet **87**.4, 19, 25, 27, 37
suicidal feelings
    after bereavement **116**.4
    children **123**.35
    helping people with **77**.1
suicide **77**.1-2, 1-5, 15-23, 32-9
    age and rates of **77**.2
    and alcohol consumption **93**.28
    bereavement by **116**.8
    and cannabis **80**.16
    as a cause of death **77**.1, 2
    and cult members **94**.21
    and depression **125**.10, 22
    effect on family and friends **77**.35, 36
    and euthanasia **102**.2
    and homeless people **79**.32
    and illness **77**.3
    inquests into **77**.1, 36-7
    men **125**.15
    prevention
        behavioural approaches **77**.3
        community-based efforts **77**.3
        environmental strategies **77**.3
        helping a suicidal friend **77**.21
        and public policy **77**.17-18
        self-help **77**.35
        students **77**.15-16, 22-3
        talking treatments **77**.35
        treatment of mental disorders **77**.3
    risk factors for **77**.2-3, 5
    and self-harm **77**.8, 9, 11, 12, 21
    social and environmental factors in **77**.3
    statistics **77**.2, 4, 16; **84**.1; **102**.4; **125**.16
    taboos surrounding **77**.2
    and university students **84**.32-3

warning signs of **77**.4

and young men **77**.1-2, 4, 17, 23, 32-3

see also assisted suicide; attempted suicide; physician-assisted suicide (PAS)

suicide bombers **92**.9, 15-16, 21

profile of **92**.16

sulphur dioxide (SO2) emissions **119**.15

supermarkets

buying patterns **43**.5

online grocery shopping **104**.5, 7

population per grocery superstore **43**.3

profits **43**.3

supermodels, and the wearing of fur **103**.36-7

supplements **118**.35

and anti-doping rules **118**.33

nutritional **118**.28

support after bereavement **116**.2, 14-15

children **116**.15, 28

support for depression sufferers **125**.18, 20

support for eating disorder sufferers **127**.25-6, 28-30

support for parents **124**.5, 6, 16-17

support for victims of bullying

children **122**.1, 2, 12, 13, 16

mobile bullying **122**.23

racist bullying **122**.4-5

workplace bullying **122**.27, 31-2, 38

surgery, and animal research **103**.3

surgical dilation and evacuation (abortion) **126**.10, 14

surveillance **82**.17-19; **120**.33-4

and facial recognition technology **82**.3

and the Government **82**.1-3, 22, 23

mass surveillance technologies **82**.1

and RFID tags **82**.16

workplace **120**.32-3

sustainable agriculture **87**.24, 35; **88**.32-3

sustainable development **20**.24; **98**.38

definition **111**.4

and global water supplies **76**.17, 31

sustainable housing **85**.1, 9

in rural areas **85**.5

and sustainable communities **85**.32, 38, 39

sustainable tourism

and ecotourism **109**.38-9

funding bodies **109**.38-9

information on **109**.28-9

T

tagging of asylum seekers **89**.36-7

tai chi **81**.3, 14, 30, 31, 39

talking therapies **125**.29-30

access to **125**.30-31

tar **86**.4, 10

in herbal cigarettes **86**.37

low tar cigarettes **86**.32

tariffs *see* trade barriers

taxation

on alcohol **93**.31, 36, 37

on aviation fuel **119**.16

carbon tax on fuel **97**.25

child tax credit (CTC) **110**.6, 7

overpayments to lone-parent families **124**.35

congestion tax **119**.34

contributions **89**.23, 30

fuel taxes **119**.14, 24

gambling **29**.2, 17, 23, 36

landfill tax **111**.3

and older people **105**.34

impact on rich and poor **110**.16

and same-sex partnerships **101**.30, 34

of tobacco **86**.7, 23, 25

technology and bullying **122**.5, 19-26

teenage pregnancies **75**.1-14, 17-27; **126**.30-31

and abortion **20**.30, 34; **75**.1, 3-4, 17; **126**.29

under 16s and confidentiality **126**.13, 28, 29

and abstinence education **75**.18, 26-7

attitudes to **75**.3, 7-8, 10, 27

and benefit cuts **75**.22

as a 'career' choice **75**.14

children of teenage mothers **75**.2, 7-8

and ethnic minorities **75**.2, 23

factors associated with **75**.2, 5

Volume numbers appear first (in bold) followed by page numbers; a change in volume number is preceded by a semi-colon.

Vol. **19** Looking at Vegetarianism
Vol. **20** Population Growth
Vol. **22** Confronting Child Abuse
Vol. **29** Gambling
Vol. **43** A Consumer Society
Vol. **60** Confronting Cancer
Vol. **69** The Media
Vol. **74** Money Matters
Vol. **75** Lone-Parent Families
Vol. **76** The Water Crisis
Vol. **77** Self-inflicted Violence
Vol. **78** Threatened Species
Vol. **79** Dealing with Homelessness
Vol. **80** The Cannabis Debate
Vol. **81** Alternative Therapies
Vol. **82** Protecting our Privacy
Vol. **83** Dealing with Crime
Vol. **84** Mental Wellbeing
Vol. **85** The Housing Crisis
Vol. **86** Smoking and your Health
Vol. **87** Genetic Modification

Vol. **88** Food and Nutrition
Vol. **89** Refugees
Vol. **90** Human and Animal Cloning
Vol. **91** Disability Issues
Vol. **92** Terrorism
Vol. **93** Binge Drinking
Vol. **94** Religions and Beliefs in Britain
Vol. **95** The Climate Crisis
Vol. **96** Preventing Sexual Diseases
Vol. **97** Energy Matters
Vol. **98** The Globalisation Issue
Vol. **99** Exploited Children
Vol. **100** Stress and Anxiety
Vol. **101** Sexuality and Discrimination
Vol. **102** The Ethics of Euthanasia
Vol. **103** Animal Rights
Vol. **104** Our Internet Society
Vol. **105** Ageing Issues
Vol. **106** Trends in Marriage
Vol. **107** Work Issues
Vol. **108** Domestic Violence

Vol. **109** Responsible Tourism
Vol. **110** Poverty
Vol. **111** The Waste Problem
Vol. **112** Women, Men and Equality
Vol. **113** Fitness and Health
Vol. **114** Drug Abuse
Vol. **115** Racial Discrimination
Vol. **116** Grief and Loss
Vol. **117** Self-Esteem and Body Image
Vol. **118** Focus on Sport
Vol. **119** Transport Trends
Vol. **120** The Human Rights Issue
Vol. **121** The Censorship Debate
Vol. **122** Bullying
Vol. **123** Young People and Health
Vol. **124** Parenting Issues
Vol. **125** Understanding Depression
Vol. **126** The Abortion Debate
Vol. **127** Eating Disorders

and family planning **20**.29-30, 34, 39
Government policies on **75**.1, 9, 13, 27
and health **75**.1, 2
international comparisons **75**.5
negative consequences of **75**.2
and poverty **75**.1, 5, 10
and sex education **75**.2-3, 13, 14, 20-22, 23
and single parents **75**.5; **126**.31
social stigma attached to **75**.10
and socio-economic background **75**.1-2
statistics **75**.1, 4; **126**.30-31
trends in **75**.4
and underage sex **75**.14, 17-18, 27
young people's attitudes to **75**.6
teenagers *see* young people
telephones
fraud **43**.26, 35
government surveillance of **82**.1, 22, 23
workplace monitoring of calls **82**.27
television **69**.1-15
advertising **69**.12, 29
public attitudes to **69**.3
alcohol advertising **93**.23
and body image **117**.11-12
children **117**.22
and childhood obesity **113**.2
children's viewing **121**.27
digital **69**.1-2
and disabled people **91**.21-2, 23-4
and political bias **69**.2
quality and standards on **69**.1, 2
offensive language **69**.2, 4, 5; **121**.38-9
reality television shows **69**.4
and sex **69**.2, 4, 5
taste and decency **69**.4-5, 17
and violence **69**.2, 4, 5, 8, 9
reality television **86**.5
promoting racial understanding **115**.22
regulation **69**.2; **121**.36-7
criticism by regulators **69**.7
watershed **121**.37, 38-9
terminally ill people
and advance directives **102**.18, 34, 37
and arguments against euthanasia **102**.13-14
and assisted suicide **102**.6, 7, 9, 15, 16, 17, 27
and freedom of choice **102**.30-1
and hospice care **102**.3-4, 13, 28, 31
and the law on euthanasia **102**.7, 8-9
and the medicinal use of cannabis **80**.37
terrorism
and aviation security **82**.3
brief history of **92**.5-8
deaths caused by **92**.34
defining **92**.1, 10-12, 19
deportation of suspects **120**.38-9
different types of **92**.2
fear of **92**.3-5, 13
and guerrilla warfare **92**.12
and identity cards **82**.2, 9, 10, 11; **120**.35
London bombings **115**.27, 36
media coverage of **92**.10, 23-4, 27, 28-9

methods of attack **92**.9, 11-12
Palestinian terrorist groups **92**.1, 2, 15-16, 20, 21
and political violence **92**.10-11, 12
testicular cancer **60**.5, 18, 26
in children **60**.11, 12, 13
tetrahydrocannabinol (THC) in cannabis **80**.2, 3, 4, 6-7, 11, 13, 15, 18, 19
and cannabis medicine **80**.39
text message bullying **122**.5, 19, 21, 22-3, 24, 25
Thalidomide, and animal research **103**.20
THC and cannabis strength **114**.37, 38
therapeutic cloning **90**.3, 5, 6, 10, 14, 17, 19, 23, 33
thermohaline circulation, and abrupt climate change **95**.18-19
Third World *see* developing countries
throat cancer **60**.15
thoughts
and healthy self-esteem **117**.30
and low self-esteem **117**.5, 6
thyroid cancer **60**.35
tidal energy **97**.2, 6, 12
time limit for abortion **126**.12, 36-8
time management, and stress **100**.27, 29, 32, 36
tissue cultures **103**.17, 19, 22
TNCs (trans-national corporations) **98**.4, 12-13
agrifood TNCs **98**.28-9, 30
and violation of human rights **98**.29
and working conditions **98**.14, 17
tobacco **114**.5, 29
additives **86**.7
consumption **86**.2
and the law **114**.32
see also smoking
tobacco companies **86**.6-7, 8, 20-1
and the hospitality trade **86**.17
profits **86**.25
tolerance to drugs **114**.2, 5, 30
torture
evidence obtained under torture **120**.39
victims **89**.18-20
tourism **98**.4
and adventure travel **109**.9-10
child sex tourism **99**.17, 20, 23, 25-6
in developing countries **20**.18
and employment **20**.18
global **109**.1-3
independent holidays **109**.8-9
Internet bookings **109**.16
UK travel trends **109**.4-5
visits to the UK **109**.6
young travellers **109**.11-15
see also ecotourism; responsible tourism
toxic chemicals
and water pollution **76**.11
trade *see* international trade
trade barriers **98**.1, 2, 9, 22
protectionism **98**.9, 10-11, 24
subsidies **98**.9, 10-11, 17, 31
trade in endangered species **78**.16-17, 19-22
and traditional medicine **78**.23
and the UK **78**.38-9

trade justice **98**.26-7, 31-2; **110**.32-3

trade unions **107**.31
    and globalisation **98**.13, 38
    and workplace stress **100**.11, 26

trading standards **88**.38-9
    and consumer complaints **43**.22-3

traffic *see* road traffic

traffic pollution *see* pollution and transport

trafficking **120**.28, 29
    and child labour **99**.1, 3, 4; **120**.18
    and the sexual exploitation of children **99**.3, 16, 17,
       20, 21, 24, 28

training
    opportunities, racial discrimination **115**.14
    and starting a business **107**.4, 34
    vocational, girls **112**.21-2
    and workplace stress **100**.16

tranquillisers
    and cocaine **114**.16
    and the law **114**.32
    and speed **114**.17

transgender people **101**.7

transplant organs
    and cloning **90**.20, 22
    xeno-transplantation **90**.30, 32-3

transport
    emissions *see* emissions. transport
    and energy efficiency **95**.5, 27, 28, 34; **97**.24, 25, 31
    public attitudes to **97**.35, 36
    standards for disabled use **91**.8, 10, 17, 25
    trends **119**.1-16, 29-31

transsexualism **101**.7

transvestism **101**.7

traumatic bereavements **116**.10-12

travel
    documents **89**.33, 35
    and gender pay gap **112**.17
    and older people **105**.28
    and terrorism
       basic advice **92**.39
       fear of **92**.3, 4, 13

treatment

acne **123**.28

chlamydia **123**.26

depression **113**.29; **123**.28; **125**.24-39

drug addiction **114**.10, 18-19

drug emergencies **114**.30

eating disorders **123**.34; **127**.28-9
    binge eating **127**.16
    bulimia **127**.14

manic depression **125**.19-20

obesity **113**.12; **127**.34
    see also weight management

post-natal depression **125**.17-18

Seasonal Affective Disorder **125**.18

tricyclics **125**.32

trips (drugs) **114**.29-30

U

underachievement, black pupils **115**.19-21

underage drinking and depression **125**.9

underage sex **123**.21
    abortion and confidentiality **126**.13, 28, 29

unemployment **98**.19-20, 32, 37; **107**.10, 37-9
    and child poverty **110**.12
    and depression, men **125**.14-15
    and homelessness **79**.12
    housing and environmental decline **85**.14
    and incapacity benefit **100**.23
    jobseekers allowance (JSA) **100**.23
    and older workers **105**.21
    and prisoners on remand **83**.26
    and teenage parenthood **75**.4

unfair dismissal, investigation of claims of, and privacy
       rights **82**.26, 27

unhealthy diet and coronary heart disease **113**.20

uniforms, schools and gender equality **112**.10-11

unipolar (endogenous) depression **84**.7; **125**.4, 10

Unitarianism **94**.2

United Reform Church **94**.2

units of alcohol **123**.16

Volume numbers appear first (in bold) followed by page numbers; a change in volume number is preceded by a semi-colon.

Vol. **19** Looking at Vegetarianism
Vol. **20** Population Growth
Vol. **22** Confronting Child Abuse
Vol. **29** Gambling
Vol. **43** A Consumer Society
Vol. **60** Confronting Cancer
Vol. **69** The Media
Vol. **74** Money Matters
Vol. **75** Lone-Parent Families
Vol. **76** The Water Crisis
Vol. **77** Self-inflicted Violence
Vol. **78** Threatened Species
Vol. **79** Dealing with Homelessness
Vol. **80** The Cannabis Debate
Vol. **81** Alternative Therapies
Vol. **82** Protecting our Privacy
Vol. **83** Dealing with Crime
Vol. **84** Mental Wellbeing
Vol. **85** The Housing Crisis
Vol. **86** Smoking and your Health
Vol. **87** Genetic Modification

Vol. **88** Food and Nutrition
Vol. **89** Refugees
Vol. **90** Human and Animal Cloning
Vol. **91** Disability Issues
Vol. **92** Terrorism
Vol. **93** Binge Drinking
Vol. **94** Religions and Beliefs in Britain
Vol. **95** The Climate Crisis
Vol. **96** Preventing Sexual Diseases
Vol. **97** Energy Matters
Vol. **98** The Globalisation Issue
Vol. **99** Exploited Children
Vol. **100** Stress and Anxiety
Vol. **101** Sexuality and Discrimination
Vol. **102** The Ethics of Euthanasia
Vol. **103** Animal Rights
Vol. **104** Our Internet Society
Vol. **105** Ageing Issues
Vol. **106** Trends in Marriage
Vol. **107** Work Issues
Vol. **108** Domestic Violence

Vol. **109** Responsible Tourism
Vol. **110** Poverty
Vol. **111** The Waste Problem
Vol. **112** Women, Men and Equality
Vol. **113** Fitness and Health
Vol. **114** Drug Abuse
Vol. **115** Racial Discrimination
Vol. **116** Grief and Loss
Vol. **117** Self-Esteem and Body Image
Vol. **118** Focus on Sport
Vol. **119** Transport Trends
Vol. **120** The Human Rights Issue
Vol. **121** The Censorship Debate
Vol. **122** Bullying
Vol. **123** Young People and Health
Vol. **124** Parenting Issues
Vol. **125** Understanding Depression
Vol. **126** The Abortion Debate
Vol. **127** Eating Disorders

universities
    admissions and exam stress **100**.7
    and animal rights activists **103**.15
    costs of a university education **74**.38
    cults recruiting from **94**.24-5
    gender differences in performance **112**.1, 8
    see also colleges; further education; students
upbringing and gender development **112**.35

V

vaccination, and life expectancy **105**.2
vaccines
    for farm livestock **19**.32
    production **87**.18
vacuum aspiration (abortion) **126**.14
vandalism
    helping to prevent **83**.35
    rates of **83**.2
    and yob-culture Britain **83**.5, 6
    young people's attitude to **83**.18
vascular diseases and depression **125**.5
veal production **19**.30, 34, 37
vegan diets **19**.1, 6, 12
    alternatives to animal products **19**.12, 13
    costs of **19**.14
    drinks **19**.14
    famous vegans **19**.12, 13
    and nutrition **19**.12, 13-14
    and protein **19**.13, 16
    and teenagers **19**.13-14
vegetables *see* fruit and vegetables
vegetarian food **19**.1
    health benefits of **19**.15, 20, 26, 33
    and healthy eating **19**.7, 9, 20
    iron-rich foods **19**.3, 8
    lacto-ovo-vegetarian **19**.1, 6
    lacto-vegetarian **19**.1
    macrobiotic **19**.1
    market value of **19**.21
    meat substitutes **19**.2, 21-2
    and nutrition **19**.3, 9
    and protein **19**.9
    pulses **19**.2
    semi or demi vegetarian **19**.1
    vegan **19**.1, 6, 12
vegetarians **19**.1-40; **88**.18
    and animal welfare **19**.6, 26, 33
    becoming a vegetarian **19**.11
    defining **19**.2, 6
    eating out **19**.2-3
    and the environment **19**.6-7, 26, 27, 33
    and foot-and-mouth disease **19**.22
    and heart disease **19**.7, 8, 16, 19, 20
    and life expectancy **105**.29
    percentage of in the population **19**.1, 21
vehicles, recycling **111**.35
verbal abuse **108**.1, 7
veterinary research **103**.10

victimisation
    and racism **115**.7-8
        at work **115**.11-12
    and religious discrimination **94**.28
    and sex discrimination **112**.14
victims of abuse **108**.1
victims of crime **83**.6
    racial identity **115**.10
    young people as **83**.7, 14
video games
    and children **121**.32-3
    and compulsive gambling **29**.37
videos
    and children **121**.26
    regulation **121**.26, 31
violence
    and advertising **69**.14
    alcohol-related **93**.1, 5, 25, 35, 36
        and children of alcoholics **93**.32, 33
    children as victims of **22**.14; **120**.17
    and computer games **121**.33, 35
    drug traffickers **114**.34
    and male depression **125**.15
    and masculinity **112**.37-8
    and mental illness **84**.4, 18
    in the media **121**.34
        effect on children **121**.28, 33, 34, 35
        and the physical punishment of children **22**.25-6
    on radio **69**.37
    on television
        and gun culture **69**.9
        public attitudes to **69**.2, 4, 5
        in soap operas **69**.4, 8, 9
violent crime
    domestic violence **83**.6
    gun crime **83**.3, 4, 18
    rates of **83**.1
    sentences for **83**.3
    surge in reports of **83**.3
    and young people **83**.15
        as victims of **83**.7
vocational education, girls **112**.21-2
volatile substance abuse (VSA) **114**.27-8
    young people **114**.21
    see also solvents
voting age, lowering **120**.7-8

W

wages
    and child domestic workers **99**.9, 10
    and consumer spending **43**.1
    footballers **118**.11
    inequality of incomes **43**.4, 13
    minimum wage **43**.4
    for students **74**.37
    see also equal pay; incomes
waist measurement and obesity **113**.11, 15
walking

as alternative to car **119**.25
health benefits of **113**.31, 39; **119**.27
to school **119**.25, 26, 27
see also exercise; pedestrians
walking bus **119**.6, 26
war and terrorism **92**.10, 11, 13
war on terror **89**.8
war-affected children **99**.32-5; **110**.36-7
and the effects of armed conflict **99**.33
help for **99**.34
problem of **99**.32
testimonials of **99**.33-4
waste
amounts **111**.5, 22, 38
collection **111**.6, 29
crime **111**.20
definitions **111**.1, 3-4
and energy generation **97**.37, 39; **111**.2, 3, 39
environmental impact **111**.1
history of **111**.5
incineration **111**.3, 6, 7, 15, 22
prevention **111**.16
reducing waste **111**.4, 17, 18
as a resource **111**.1
and water consumption **76**.1, 4, 19, 32, 36
in the workplace **111**.18
see also household waste; landfill; litter; organic waste;
recycling
waste hierarchy **111**.1, 4
wastelands, and wildlife in London **85**.16-17
water abstraction, and wildlife **76**.34
water companies **88**.31
contact with schools **76**.1
multinational water corporations **76**.22, 23, 29-30
responsibilities of **76**.1
and water bills in the UK **76**.33
and water conservation **76**.36
water conservation **76**.1, 3, 22, 37-9
answering questions about **76**.36
in everyday life **76**.27
in the garden **76**.1, 36, 37, 38
in the home **76**.37, 38

investment in **76**.27
in schools **76**.39
and showers **76**.1, 27, 37, 38
and toilet flushing **76**.2, 27, 37, 38
water consumption
bottled water **76**.23, 27
and eco-systems **76**.2, 16-17, 19
groundwater sources for drinking **76**.7, 9, 12
and the importance of water quality **76**.9
lack of access to clean water **76**.8, 9
largest users of water **76**.36
per capita household water consumption by region
76.26
and population growth **76**.22, 29
reasons for growth in **76**.3, 5, 8
in selected countries **76**.7
statistics **76**.7, 9
and waste **76**.1, 4, 19, 32, 36
water requirements per person per day **76**.6
and water shortages **76**.21-2
water cycle **76**.2, 21
water management
and agriculture **76**.18
costs of **76**.33
dealing with the water crisis **76**.22, 26-8
government and planned policies of **76**.8-9, 17
and multinational water corporations **76**.29-30
pricing mechanisms **76**.22, 32
and privatisation **76**.22-3, 32
and wars over the ownership of water resources **76**.22
water meters **76**.36, 38
water pollution **76**.1, 5, 10-11
causes of **76**.4, 7, 8, 9
in the developed world **76**.10-11
in developing countries **76**.4, 10
and global water supplies **76**.10-11, 15
and multinational water corporations **76**.29-30
statistics **76**.9
and water shortages **76**.36
water stress, calculating **76**.15-16, 17
water supplies **76**.15-17; **98**.26
and climate change **95**.1, 3, 7, 11, 12, 13, 15, 17, 26

Volume numbers appear first (in bold) followed by page numbers; a change in volume number is preceded by a semi-colon.

Vol. **19** Looking at Vegetarianism
Vol. **20** Population Growth
Vol. **22** Confronting Child Abuse
Vol. **29** Gambling
Vol. **43** A Consumer Society
Vol. **60** Confronting Cancer
Vol. **69** The Media
Vol. **74** Money Matters
Vol. **75** Lone-Parent Families
Vol. **76** The Water Crisis
Vol. **77** Self-inflicted Violence
Vol. **78** Threatened Species
Vol. **79** Dealing with Homelessness
Vol. **80** The Cannabis Debate
Vol. **81** Alternative Therapies
Vol. **82** Protecting our Privacy
Vol. **83** Dealing with Crime
Vol. **84** Mental Wellbeing
Vol. **85** The Housing Crisis
Vol. **86** Smoking and your Health
Vol. **87** Genetic Modification

Vol. **88** Food and Nutrition
Vol. **89** Refugees
Vol. **90** Human and Animal Cloning
Vol. **91** Disability Issues
Vol. **92** Terrorism
Vol. **93** Binge Drinking
Vol. **94** Religions and Beliefs in Britain
Vol. **95** The Climate Crisis
Vol. **96** Preventing Sexual Diseases
Vol. **97** Energy Matters
Vol. **98** The Globalisation Issue
Vol. **99** Exploited Children
Vol. **100** Stress and Anxiety
Vol. **101** Sexuality and Discrimination
Vol. **102** The Ethics of Euthanasia
Vol. **103** Animal Rights
Vol. **104** Our Internet Society
Vol. **105** Ageing Issues
Vol. **106** Trends in Marriage
Vol. **107** Work Issues
Vol. **108** Domestic Violence

Vol. **109** Responsible Tourism
Vol. **110** Poverty
Vol. **111** The Waste Problem
Vol. **112** Women, Men and Equality
Vol. **113** Fitness and Health
Vol. **114** Drug Abuse
Vol. **115** Racial Discrimination
Vol. **116** Grief and Loss
Vol. **117** Self-Esteem and Body Image
Vol. **118** Focus on Sport
Vol. **119** Transport Trends
Vol. **120** The Human Rights Issue
Vol. **121** The Censorship Debate
Vol. **122** Bullying
Vol. **123** Young People and Health
Vol. **124** Parenting Issues
Vol. **125** Understanding Depression
Vol. **126** The Abortion Debate
Vol. **127** Eating Disorders

financing the provision of **76**.31-2
and food production **76**.3, 4, 7, 18
and livestock cultivation **19**.7
and multinational water corporations **76**.29-30
and planned water management policies **76**.8-9, 17
and population growth **20**.6, 9, 13-14, 22, 23, 24
projected worldwide water use **76**.35
statistics **76**.1, 2, 4, 6, 8, 19, 20
and tourism **109**.30
and water as a human right **76**.24-5, 32
and water pollution **76**.10-11, 15
and water shortages **76**.15-17, 19, 21-2
water usage by sector **76**.3
and water users **76**.36
water vapour emissions
aircraft **119**.16
and global warming **95**.1, 8, 15
watershed, television **121**.37
erosion of **121**.38-9
wave power **97**.2, 6, 12
We the Children report **120**.3
wealth
children, UK **110**.10
and cultural poverty **110**.22-3
diseases of **110**.35
and obesity **113**.12
and segregation **115**.32
women **112**.19
weapons testing, animal experiments in **103**.1
weather patterns
and climate change **95**.2-3, 5, 7, 9, 11, 12, 15, 16, 25;
  97.1
abrupt **95**.19
website bullying **122**.20, 21
weddings rings, history of **106**.20
weed control **87**.9, 19, 25
weight *see* body weight; obesity
weight concerns, young people **123**.1
weight loss rate **113**.27
weight management **113**.12, 31-2, 33; **127**.34
children **113**.7-8
and exercise **113**.34, 39
weight monitoring in schools **127**.36
weight perceptions, adults **113**.13
weight problems *see* obesity; underweight people
welfare support *see* State benefits
West Antarctic ice sheet (WAIS) **95**.12, 13, 19
Western society and female body image **117**.16-17
whales
hunting **78**.6, 13, 14
watching **78**.13-14
wheat (GM) **87**.19, 34
wheelchair students **91**.36
Whitehouse, Mary **121**.36
wholegrain foods **88**.15
widowed people, suicide attacks by **92**.15
wild animals
in animal experiments **103**.6
and the fur trade **103**.38-9
wildflowers, threatened species in Britain **78**.36
wildlife

captive breeding **78**.22
conservation **88**.32, 34
and the exotic pet trade **78**.21-2
crime **78**.19, 38-9
illegal trade in **78**.21-2; **109**.39
killing of **78**.2, 4-5, 5-6
and the law **78**.16-17, 38-9
in London **85**.16-17
and new house-building in the south-east **85**.33
overcollecting **78**.22
impact of paper recycling **111**.32
and population growth **20**.6, 8-9, 14, 21, 22
rare species **78**.28
tourism **109**.29, 38
trade in live animals **78**.20-1
vulnerable species **78**.28
and water abstraction **76**.34, 36
see also conservation; endangered species; extinction
wills **74**.16
Wilms' tumours **60**.9, 11
wind energy **97**.2, 4, 5, 6, 9, 21, 38
and climate change **97**.15
costs of **97**.16
energy available from **97**.5
new wind farm projects **97**.5
and noise **97**.17
numbers of wind farms **97**.11
offshore **97**.12, 16, 26
opposition to wind farms **97**.12
public attitudes to **97**.16
top myths about **97**.15-17
turbines **97**.5, 15, 17, 38
in the UK **97**.13, 26
wind power **95**.29, 34
wine
consumption, young people **123**.1
expenditure on **43**.2
winter deaths, older people **110**.19
withdrawal from drugs **114**.5
witnessing bullying **122**.1-2
womb cancer **60**.5
women
and abortion
decision-making **126**.16
rights **126**.21
views on abortion time limit **126**.36, 37-8
and ageism **105**.16
and alcohol
binge drinking **93**.1, 10, 12, 18, 19-20
and brain function **93**.26
consumption **93**.10
deaths from liver disease **93**.11
drinking above recommended guidelines **93**.18, 35
effects of **93**.13
'female friendly' bars **93**.10
health benefits of **93**.9, 28, 30
and hospital admissions **93**.9, 19
pregnant women **93**.4, 27
safe limits **93**.2, 3, 4, 27, 29, 38
young women **93**.1, 15, 16, 19-20
and body image *see* body image, women

and cancer **60**.3, 4, 5, 27
    cervical cancer **60**.5, 14, 16
    lung cancer **60**.15
and child abuse **22**.3, 4, 6, 10, 33
childless **20**.26
in construction industry **112**.25
and debt problems **43**.30-1, 38-9
decline in single older women **43**.2
in developing countries **20**.2, 3, 9, 20
discrimination against older women **105**.16, 21-2
employment prospects **107**.32
equality and child labour **99**.12
and exercise **113**.23, 27, 28
expenditure on toiletries **43**.2
and family planning **20**.25, 26, 27, 29-30
and fertility *see* fertility treatment; infertility
and the future of work **107**.12
and gambling **29**.3, 8
gender pay gap **107**.13, 25, 26; **112**.16-17
glass cliff/glass ceiling **107**.9; **112**.15-16, 20
and higher education **112**.8
and HIV/AIDS **96**.20, 24-5, 29, 30-1
and homelessness **79**.10
and the Internet **104**.12
iron deficiency in **19**.5
job satisfaction **112**.22-3
life expectancy **105**.2, 9, 19
maternal mortality **20**.25, 28, 29, 30, 36, 37, 39
maternity leave **107**.16, 21
and mental illness **84**.1
missing persons **79**.13
and part-time working **107**.17
post-natal depression **125**.4, 17-18
and poverty
    global **110**.22
    in the UK **110**.11, 17-18, 19
pregnant women **88**.7
pregnant women and cannabis **80**.15, 19
prisoners **83**.9
rough sleepers **79**.10
and self-injury **77**.12-14
and sexually transmitted infections (STIs) **96**.3, 9

single **106**.3, 20
single homeless **79**.19
and smoking **60**.27; **86**.1, 2, 5, 9, 14, 24, 25, 38, 154
in sport **118**.18-20, 21-2
and stress **100**.13
    frequent worrying **100**.19
and suicidal thoughts **77**.2
suicide attacks by **92**.15
and suicide rates **77**.2
and vegetarianism **19**.1
wealth **112**.19
working mothers **107**.26
working in the tourist industry **109**.33
see also girls and young women; infertility; mothers;
    pregnancy;
working mothers
women in the workforce **112**.12, 20
    equal pay *see* equal pay
    and the 'glass ceiling' **112**.15-16, 20
    managers **112**.18
    non-traditional careers **112**.21, 25-7
    and the pay gap **112**.16-17, 20
    and the UK labour market **112**.12
    see also working mothers
wood recycling **111**.36
woodland burial grounds **116**.39
words to describe racial identity **115**.4-5
work
    absenteeism and obesity **113**.17
    exploitation of workers **120**.28-31
    see also child labour; slavery
work and gender *see* gender and work
work-family balance **112**.37, 38
work-life balance **107**.6, 14, 16
    and age **105**.24
    see also hours of work
workaholism **107**.29
working abroad **107**.3
working conditions **98**.4, 13, 14, 17, 25-6
    in the tourist industry **109**.30, 31, 32
working days, lost through alcohol-related absences **93**.35
working hours *see* hours of work

Volume numbers appear first (in bold) followed by page numbers; a change in volume number is preceded by a semi-colon.

Vol. **19** Looking at Vegetarianism
Vol. **20** Population Growth
Vol. **22** Confronting Child Abuse
Vol. **29** Gambling
Vol. **43** A Consumer Society
Vol. **60** Confronting Cancer
Vol. **69** The Media
Vol. **74** Money Matters
Vol. **75** Lone-Parent Families
Vol. **76** The Water Crisis
Vol. **77** Self-inflicted Violence
Vol. **78** Threatened Species
Vol. **79** Dealing with Homelessness
Vol. **80** The Cannabis Debate
Vol. **81** Alternative Therapies
Vol. **82** Protecting our Privacy
Vol. **83** Dealing with Crime
Vol. **84** Mental Wellbeing
Vol. **85** The Housing Crisis
Vol. **86** Smoking and your Health
Vol. **87** Genetic Modification

Vol. **88** Food and Nutrition
Vol. **89** Refugees
Vol. **90** Human and Animal Cloning
Vol. **91** Disability Issues
Vol. **92** Terrorism
Vol. **93** Binge Drinking
Vol. **94** Religions and Beliefs in Britain
Vol. **95** The Climate Crisis
Vol. **96** Preventing Sexual Diseases
Vol. **97** Energy Matters
Vol. **98** The Globalisation Issue
Vol. **99** Exploited Children
Vol. **100** Stress and Anxiety
Vol. **101** Sexuality and Discrimination
Vol. **102** The Ethics of Euthanasia
Vol. **103** Animal Rights
Vol. **104** Our Internet Society
Vol. **105** Ageing Issues
Vol. **106** Trends in Marriage
Vol. **107** Work Issues
Vol. **108** Domestic Violence

Vol. **109** Responsible Tourism
Vol. **110** Poverty
Vol. **111** The Waste Problem
Vol. **112** Women, Men and Equality
Vol. **113** Fitness and Health
Vol. **114** Drug Abuse
Vol. **115** Racial Discrimination
Vol. **116** Grief and Loss
Vol. **117** Self-Esteem and Body Image
Vol. **118** Focus on Sport
Vol. **119** Transport Trends
Vol. **120** The Human Rights Issue
Vol. **121** The Censorship Debate
Vol. **122** Bullying
Vol. **123** Young People and Health
Vol. **124** Parenting Issues
Vol. **125** Understanding Depression
Vol. **126** The Abortion Debate
Vol. **127** Eating Disorders

working mothers **107**.26
working parents **107**.21-2, 24-5, 26
    effect on families **124**.1, 21
    role of father **124**.7-8, 11
workophiles **107**.2
workplace
    and cannabis users **80**.22
    and disabled people **91**.15-16
    dismissals
        reasons for **82**.28
        unfair **82**.26, 27
    and energy efficiency **95**.32
    gender equality, and men **112**.36-7
    and healthy eating **113**.18
    and Internet addiction **104**.37
    and mental health **84**.23
    and personal emails **104**.15
    and privacy rights **82**.25-30
        and CCTV **82**.26, 27
        company policies on electronic communications **82**.30
        European-level regulation of **82**.28
        personal information **82**.30
    racism **115**.11-14
    segregation and pay gap **112**.17
    smoking **86**.17, 18, 19, 23, 25
    surveillance **120**.32-3
    travel plans **119**.32-3
    waste **111**.18
    working conditions **98**.4, 13, 14, 17, 25-6
workplace bullying **122**.27-39
    anti-bullying policies **122**.39
    avoiding **122**.35
    defining **122**.27, 28, 37
    effects **122**.30, 31, 33, 37-8
    and harassment **122**.30
    responses to **122**.27, 31-2, 33, 37-8
    signs **122**.27, 28-9, 37, 39
    and small businesses **122**.36
    support **122**.31-2, 38
World Anti-Doping Agency (WADA) **118**.25, 27
World Anti-Doping Code **118**.27, 31-2
World Bank **98**.1-2, 3, 7-8
    organisational structure **98**.7
    origins **98**.7
    project failure rate **98**.7
    and world debt **110**.27
world debt **110**.27-8
World Fit for Children, A **120**.3
World Fit for Us, A children's forum **120**.3
World Summit for Children **120**.3
world trade *see* international trade
World Trade Organisation (WTO) **87**.6; **88**.33
    enforcement of trade rules **98**.27
    and global water supplies **76**.5, 23
    and globalisation **98**.3, 9-10, 17, 21-3
    and the liberalisation of water **76**.29
World Wide Web (WWW) **104**.2
    browsers **104**.2
    pharming websites **104**.33-4
    phishing websites **104**.32-3

worries, young people **123**.2-3

X

X-linked inactivation **90**.37
xeno-transplantation **90**.30, 32-3, 35

Y

Yahoo and Chinese censorship **121**.19
yob-culture Britain **83**.5-6
yoga **81**.3, 30, 39
    and exam stress **100**.5
young children
    gender differences in achievements **112**.7
    obesity **113**.3
young offenders and mental health problems **84**.1, 28-9
young parents and non-traditional families **124**.20-21
young people
    and abortion **126**.13, 17-18, 28-9
      confidentiality **126**.13, 28, 29
      telling parents **126**.28, 29
      views on abortion for disability **126**.35
    affordable housing for **85**.3-4
    and age discrimination **105**.16, 24
    attitudes to global poverty **110**.24
    attitudes to Islam and terrorism **92**.36
    attitudes to marriage **106**.5
    attitudes to work **105**.23
    bereavement support **116**.28
    and cannabis **80**.3, 18
      and the cannabis economy **80**.8-9
      Government policies on **80**.25, 26
      and mental illness **80**.17
      under 18s and the police **80**.7, 25, 30, 31, 34
    as consumers **43**.6-7
    and contraception **123**.22; **126**.23
    and depression **123**.27-8; **125**.8, 9
    in developing countries **20**.10-11, 33-4, 40
    and divorce **124**.29-30, 34
    and drug abuse **114**.20-28; **123**.14
    and driving **114**.23-4
    and eating disorders **123**.33-4
    and emotional problems **123**.10
    and funerals **116**.23
    and gambling **29**.2, 37-8; **43**.24
      compulsive gambling **29**.2, 19, 37-8
    going missing **79**.13-14
    and grief **116**.19-28
    health-related behaviour **123**.1-3
    and healthy eating **88**.4
    and HIV/AIDS **96**.17, 24-9, 38
    homelessness *see* homeless young people
    house prices and first-time buyers **85**.6, 7
    and identity (ID) cards, opposition to **82**.7
    and the Internet **104**.3-5, 9-11, 13, 17-29
    and iron deficiency **19**.5

and justice system **120**.1-2, 12-13
and mental health **123**.9; **125**.16
and mental illness **84**.1, 5-6
 and education **84**.30-2
 in the family **84**.8-10
 schizophrenia **84**.13-15
 seeking help **84**.28
 symptoms of emotional and behavioural disorders
  84.30-1
and money matters **74**.1-4, 14-17
 attitudes to money **74**.2
 budgeting **74**.2, 3, 14-15, 23
 credit cards **74**.15, 16
 debt **74**.1, 2, 15, 16, 23-4
 and insurance **74**.2, 15
 paying bills **74**.2
 pension planning **74**.1-2
 savings **74**.15
 teenagers **74**.8-9
and nutrition **123**.1, 6-7
and obesity **123**.31
parenting teenage children **124**.16-17
and pregnancy *see* teenage pregnancies
and religion **94**.6-7
rights **120**.1-22
and self-harm **77**.6-7, 9, 14; **123**.36-9
and sex **123**.19-21
sexual exploitation of teenagers **99**.20-2
sexual health **20**.33-4, 40
and sexually transmitted infections (STIs) **96**.3, 4,
 8-9, 25; **123**.25-6
and shopping on the Internet **43**.23-4
as single parents **126**.31
and smoking **123**.11-13
and sport **118**.2
and suicide **77**.1-2, 4-5, 17; **84**.1; **123**.35
teenage girls
 body image **117**.20-21
 and domestic violence **108**.29
 eating habits **117**.20
 plastic surgery **117**.26-8
teenage smoking **86**.1, 2, 5-7

and vegan diets **19**.13-14
and vegetarian diets **19**.1
voting rights **120**.7-8
worry about getting older **105**.8
young people and alcohol **93**.12-17; **123**.1-2, 9, 14-19
 attitudes to **93**.16, 17
 binge drinking **93**.1, 6, 10, 12, 16
 drinking habits **93**.12, 39; **123**.1-2, 19
 eating problems **127**.20-21
 education about **93**.11, 16
 effects of **93**.6-7, 13, 24; **123**.15
 getting help **123**.14
 and HIV **96**.26
 hospital admissions for alcohol abuse **93**.15
 influence of others **93**.16-17
 and the law **93**.6, 11; **123**.16
 problems **123**.18-19
 risks **123**.14
 in rural areas **93**.12, 14
 safety information **93**.13; **123**.16, 17
 statistics **123**.1-2
 under-age drinking **93**.6, 15, 25, 35, 36, 39
young people and sexuality
 coming out **101**.11-13, 17
 exploring **101**.1
 and the law **101**.3, 27
Young People into 2006 report **123**.1-3
Your Shout About Africa survey **110**.24
youth detention centres, restraint techniques **120**.17
youth justice **120**.12, 13

Z

Zealots (early Jewish terrorists) **92**.1, 6, 7
zebra fish **90**.32
Zen Buddhism, and Kinhin (walking meditation) **100**.10
Zen macrobiotic diets **19**.1
zinc **88**.6
zoo conservation **78**.24-5
Zoroastrians **94**.3

Volume numbers appear first (in bold) followed by page numbers; a change in volume number is preceded by a semi-colon.

Vol. **19** Looking at Vegetarianism
Vol. **20** Population Growth
Vol. **22** Confronting Child Abuse
Vol. **29** Gambling
Vol. **43** A Consumer Society
Vol. **60** Confronting Cancer
Vol. **69** The Media
Vol. **74** Money Matters
Vol. **75** Lone-Parent Families
Vol. **76** The Water Crisis
Vol. **77** Self-inflicted Violence
Vol. **78** Threatened Species
Vol. **79** Dealing with Homelessness
Vol. **80** The Cannabis Debate
Vol. **81** Alternative Therapies
Vol. **82** Protecting our Privacy
Vol. **83** Dealing with Crime
Vol. **84** Mental Wellbeing
Vol. **85** The Housing Crisis
Vol. **86** Smoking and your Health
Vol. **87** Genetic Modification

Vol. **88** Food and Nutrition
Vol. **89** Refugees
Vol. **90** Human and Animal Cloning
Vol. **91** Disability Issues
Vol. **92** Terrorism
Vol. **93** Binge Drinking
Vol. **94** Religions and Beliefs in Britain
Vol. **95** The Climate Crisis
Vol. **96** Preventing Sexual Diseases
Vol. **97** Energy Matters
Vol. **98** The Globalisation Issue
Vol. **99** Exploited Children
Vol. **100** Stress and Anxiety
Vol. **101** Sexuality and Discrimination
Vol. **102** The Ethics of Euthanasia
Vol. **103** Animal Rights
Vol. **104** Our Internet Society
Vol. **105** Ageing Issues
Vol. **106** Trends in Marriage
Vol. **107** Work Issues
Vol. **108** Domestic Violence

Vol. **109** Responsible Tourism
Vol. **110** Poverty
Vol. **111** The Waste Problem
Vol. **112** Women, Men and Equality
Vol. **113** Fitness and Health
Vol. **114** Drug Abuse
Vol. **115** Racial Discrimination
Vol. **116** Grief and Loss
Vol. **117** Self-Esteem and Body Image
Vol. **118** Focus on Sport
Vol. **119** Transport Trends
Vol. **120** The Human Rights Issue
Vol. **121** The Censorship Debate
Vol. **122** Bullying
Vol. **123** Young People and Health
Vol. **124** Parenting Issues
Vol. **125** Understanding Depression
Vol. **126** The Abortion Debate
Vol. **127** Eating Disorders